PLAN® ENGLISH
TEST PREPARATION GUIDE

MAY 2012

Author: Mallory Grantham

Project Coordinator: Zuzana Urbanek

Contributing Writer:
Brittany Rowland

American Book Company
PO Box 2638
Woodstock, GA 30188-1383
Toll Free: 1 (888) 264-5877   Phone: (770) 928-2834
Toll Free Fax: 1 (866) 827-3240
website: www.americanbookcompany.com

ACKNOWLEDGEMENTS

The authors would like to gratefully acknowledge the technical contributions of Marsha Torrens and Becky Wright, as well as the proofreading expertise of Susan Barrows.

The authors would also like to thank Mary Stoddard for designing the original icon.

© 2012 American Book Company
PO Box 2638
Woodstock, GA 30188-1318

ALL RIGHTS RESERVED

The text of this publication, or any part thereof, may not be reproduced or transmitted in any form or by any means, electronic or mechanical, including photocopying, recording, storage in an information retrieval system, or otherwise, without the prior written permission of the publisher.

Printed in the United States of America

05/12

Preface v

Diagnostic Test 1
Diagnostic Test Evaluation Chart 14

Chapter 1 Preparing for the PLAN English Test 15
The PLAN English Test 15
Frequently Asked Questions 16
Tips for PLAN Preparation and Testing 17
    Preparing for the PLAN 17
    Taking the PLAN 17
What to Look for When You Take the PLAN English Test 18
    How the PLAN English Test Will Look 19
        Sample Passage 19
        Sample Questions and Explanations 19
Going Forward 23

Chapter 2 Topic, Purpose, and Focus 25
Focus 26
    Focused Main Idea 26
Purpose 32
Chapter 2 Summary 39
Chapter 2 Review 39

Chapter 3 Organization, Unity, and Coherence 43
Paragraphs 44
Developing Coherence 47
Organizing Ideas 47
    Using Transitions 49
        Sequence of Events 49
        Cause-Effect 50
        Compare and Contrast 50

  Using Conjunctive Adverbs 50
 Chapter 3 Summary 54
 Chapter 3 Review 54

Chapter 4 Word Choice — 57

 Writing with Style 58
  Choosing the Right Words 60
 Tone and Mood 63
 Clarity 65
  Revising Awkward Sentences 65
  Avoiding Vague Pronouns 66
  Using Logical Conjunctions 67
 Economy 69
 Chapter 4 Summary 72
 Chapter 4 Review 73

Chapter 5 Sentence Structure — 77

 Sentences 77
  Sentence Errors 78
 Modifiers 83
 Errors in Construction 86
  Shifts in Verb Tense 86
  Shifts in Person 86
  Missing or Incorrect Relative Pronouns 87
 Chapter 5 Summary 90
 Chapter 5 Review 91

Chapter 6 Usage — 93

 Grammar and Usage 93
 Verbs 94
  Verb Tenses 95
  Irregular Verbs 96
  Subject-Verb Agreement 97
 Pronouns 100
  Reflexive Pronouns 101
  Relative Pronouns 102
  Pronoun Agreement 102
 Adjectives and Adverbs 105
  Comparative and Superlative Modifiers 105
 Prepositions 107
 Frequently Confused Word Pairs 109
 Chapter 6 Summary 112
 Chapter 6 Review 113

Chapter 7 Punctuation — 117

- End Punctuation 118
- Internal Punctuation 119
  - Commas 119
  - Apostrophes 122
  - Colons 122
  - Semicolons 123
- Chapter 7 Summary 126
- Chapter 7 Review 127

Practice Test 1 — 129

Practice Test 2 — 145

Index — 161

Preface

The *PLAN® English Test Preparation Guide* will help students preparing to take the PLAN English Test. The most up-to-date requirements and strategies for the PLAN English Test are covered in this book. PLAN® is a registered trademark of ACT series, Inc. American Book Company is not affiliated with ACT, Inc., and produced this book independently.

This book contains several sections: 1) general information about the book, 2) a complete diagnostic reading test, 3) an evaluation chart, 4) chapters that review the strategies, concepts, and skills that improve readiness for the PLAN English Test, and 5) two complete practice English tests. Answers to the practice tests, chapter practices, and chapter reviews are in a separate manual.

We welcome comments and suggestions about the book. Please contact the authors at

American Book Company
PO Box 2638
Woodstock, GA 30188-1383

Toll Free: 1 (888) 264-5877
Phone: (770) 928-2834
Fax: (770) 928-7483
Website: www.americanbookcompany.com

Preface

About the Authors:

Mallory Grantham is an ELA writer and copy editor at American Book Company. She completed her Bachelor of Arts in English at Kennesaw State University. As a teaching assistant, she led lectures, created lesson plans, graded and edited papers, and evaluated student progress. In addition, Mallory has taught sign language and tutored students in English and mathematics.

Brittany Rowland graduated from Kennesaw State University with a master's degree in professional writing. As a substitute teacher, she has taught English and literature to high school students. Additionally, Brittany has written short fiction and worked as a content writer for developing websites.

About the Project Coordinator:

Zuzana Urbanek served as ELA Curriculum Coordinator for American Book Company. She is a professional writer and editor with over twenty-five years of experience in education, business, and publishing. She has taught a variety of English courses at the college level and also has taught English as a foreign language abroad. Her master's degree is from Arizona State University.

Diagnostic Test

30 Minutes – 50 Questions

Directions: Read the following passages. In each passage, certain words and phrases are underlined and numbered. In the right-hand column, you will find alternative choices for the underlined part. Choose the answer that best expresses the idea, makes the statement appropriate for standard written English, or is worded most consistently with the style and tone of the passage as a whole. If you think the original version is best, choose NO CHANGE. In some cases, there will be in the right-hand column a question about the underlined part. Choose the best answer to the question.

There might also be questions about a section of the passage or about the passage as a whole. These questions do not refer to an underlined portion of the passage; they are identified by a number or numbers in a box.

For each question, choose the best answer, and circle the corresponding letter of your answer. Remember that for many of the questions, you must read several sentences beyond the question to determine the answer. Be sure that you have read far enough ahead each time you choose an answer.

Diagnostic Test
Would You Like to Live Forever?

[1]

How would you like to see the twenty-second century? This sounds like a far-fetched dream, but right now, researchers are working in labs all over the world pursuing an objective straight out of science fiction. Their goal is to double the human lifespan from 77 to 150 years!

[2]

Take for instance, the analogy of a car. Most people expect to use a car for about ten years, and then discard it because its not running as well as when it was new. But what about the cars built in the 1940s and '50s that are still running on the road today? The difference is simple: it's all in the maintenance.

1. **A.** NO CHANGE
   B. Its goal are
   C. Their goals is
   D. It's goals are

2. **F.** NO CHANGE
   G. Take, the analogy for instance, of a car
   H. For instance, take the analogy, of a car
   J. Take, for instance, the analogy of a car

3. **A.** NO CHANGE
   B. because it's not running as well
   C. because its' not running as well
   D. because its's not running as well

4. **F.** NO CHANGE
   G. difference is simple; It's all
   H. difference is simple: It's all
   J. difference is simple, it's all

Diagnostic Test

[3]

A well-tended car requires constant attention on the part of the owner to maintain a like-new condition. The conscientious car owner <u>tweaked</u> a change in the engine's
 5
 timing back into line or replaces a worn belt. He keeps tires properly inflated and keeps oil and other fluids within their optimum ranges. The result is a showpiece of <u>steel and chrome.</u>
 6
<u>Still operating at peak efficiency</u> far beyond the accepted limit of its lifespan.

[4]

The new bioengineers view the human body <u>the same exact way</u>. The American <u>diet,</u>
 7   8
<u>full of fats sugars, and sodium, stresses</u> your body's cells and makes them age faster. Another problem contributing to American's bad health is the convenience of fast-food restaurants. <u>With wise preventive</u>
                                                        9
<u>maintenance, damage</u> to cells can be repaired long before it results in cellular death or mutation.

5. A. NO CHANGE
    B. tweaking
    C. will tweak
    D. tweaks

6. F. NO CHANGE
    G. steel and chrome that still operates at peak efficiency
    H. steel and chrome; still operating at peak efficiency
    J. steel and chrome, still operates at peak efficiency

7. A. NO CHANGE
    B. the exact same way
    C. the similar way
    D. the same way

8. F. NO CHANGE
    G. diet, full of fats, sugars, and sodium, stresses
    H. diet, full of fats sugars and sodium, stresses
    J. diet; full of fats, sugars, and sodium; stresses

9. A. NO CHANGE
    B. With wise, preventive, maintenance damage
    C. With wise preventive, maintenance, damage
    D. With, wise preventive maintenance, damage

Keeping the right nutritional balance not only protects cells, but it also boosts the immune system and maintains proper organ function. [10]

[5]

You have the advantage here. It's early in the game, and you haven't run yourself ragged. If you start taking care of your body as you would a fine piece of machinery, the chances are good that you'll be ringing in the year 2100—and beyond!

10. Which of the following sentences from Paragraph 4 is irrelevant to the passage and should be removed?
    F. NO CHANGE
    G. The new bioengineers view the human body the same way.
    H. Another problem contributing to American's bad health is the convenience of fast-food restaurants.
    J. Keeping the right nutritional balance not only protects cells, but it also boosts the immune system and maintains proper organ function.

11. A. NO CHANGE
    B. you have not worn your machine out
    C. you have not been ever so hard on yourself
    D. you haven't particularly tired your body to its extent

Question 12 asks about the preceding passage as a whole.

12. Suppose that the writer wanted to add the following detail to the essay:

    Any natural wear and tear is rectified before the car's overall condition worsens.

    This sentence would most logically fit into:
    F. Paragraph 1.
    G. Paragraph 3.
    H. the beginning of Paragraph 4.
    J. the end of Paragraph 5.

Diagnostic Test

Boudicca, Warrior Queen of the Britons

[1]

In ancient times, the Roman Empire reigned supreme. As they conquered new territories, Romans brought engineering and architecture, law and government, and sewer systems and road building. The primitive peoples, awed by the Romans, was easy to dominate.
                                            13

[2]

Boudicca ruled a Celtic tribe. Ancient Britain was a jigsaw puzzle of small kingdoms. The native Britons quarreled more between themselves than with their Roman overlords. Through treaties, the occupying Romans allowed the Britons, to keep some
                                14
power; or upon the death of Boudicca's
       15
husband, his treaty was over. The Romans seized his kingdom and smacked around
                                    16
Boudicca and her daughters, who were left to
                    17
serve as living examples of Rome's power.

13. A. NO CHANGE
    B. people, awed by the Romans, was
    C. peoples, awed by the Romans, were
    D. persons, awed by the Romans, was

14. F. NO CHANGE
    G. allowed the Britons to keep some power
    H. allowed the Britons to keep, some power
    J. allowed, the Britons, to keep some power

15. A. NO CHANGE
    B. for
    C. but
    D. so

16. F. NO CHANGE
    G. horribly pounded
    H. badly beat up
    J. brutally tortured

17. A. NO CHANGE
    B. her daughters, that were left to serve
    C. her daughters who were left, to serve
    D. her daughters which were left to serve

[3]

Rome had angered the wrong person. Boudicca traveled by chariot to all the kingdoms of Britain. Shamed by Boudicca's righteous anger, the other kings united. A mighty army formed, made up of angry Britons bent <u>up</u> driving the Romans from their land. [19]
        18

[4]

Boudicca planned a surprise attack. Her allies, the Druids, staged a revolt on a distant island to distract the Roman legions. <u>While</u> the Romans marched to the west coast of
        20
Britain, Boudicca and thousands of Britons rose in the east. Her armies slaughtered 5,000 soldiers of the powerful ninth Roman legion. The successful Britons <u>marched on. Sacking and burning</u> Roman settlements. A Roman
        21
writer estimated that Boudicca's armies killed some 70,000 Romans.

18. F. NO CHANGE
    G. out
    H. in
    J. on

19. The author wants to add this sentence to Paragraph 3:

    She displayed her sickening scars to the shocked Britons and challenged them to unite and fight like men for their homeland.

    Based on the purpose of the passage, would this be a good addition to make?

    A. No, because it takes away from the focus on the Roman Empire in the passage.
    B. Yes, because it gives descriptive details of Boudicca's physical pain from the ordeal.
    C. No, because it shows the other kings are not as important to this passage as Boudicca is.
    D. Yes, because it gives relevant details as to how Boudicca gained support from other kings.

20. F. NO CHANGE
    G. Until
    H. Instead
    J. Then

21. A. NO CHANGE
    B. marched on; sacking and burning
    C. marched on, sacking and burning
    D. marched on, and sacking and burning

[5]

The Roman military governor was startlingly alarmed. This woman had become a major threat. He plotted to capture her. He finally trapped Boudicca's forces, and they were wiped out.

[6]

Boudicca escaped—but rather than be taken prisoner, she herself took her own life. With her death, the rebellion was quelled.

22. F. NO CHANGE
G. alarmed
H. startling
J. startled

Questions 23 and 24 ask about the preceding passage as a whole.

23. What is the main topic of this passage?
    A. Why the Romans had conquered the Celts
    B. How Boudicca waged war against the Romans
    C. How the Romans were ashamed of the Britons
    D. Why the Druids helped Boudicca in her attacks

24. Suppose that the writer wanted to add the following sentence to the essay:

    Boudicca passed into British folklore as a great hero.

    This sentence would most logically fit into:
    F. the beginning of Paragraph 1.
    G. the end of Paragraph 2.
    H. the beginning of Paragraph 4.
    J. the end of Paragraph 6.

Sea Lampreys Are on the Loose!

[1]

[1] It is <u>Petromyzon marinus; the sea lamprey</u>. [2] What is forty inches long with one nostril, two eyes, fourteen gills, and dozens of razor-sharp teeth? [3] That is where the <u>lampreys impact is</u> being felt the most.
[4] As their name suggests, sea lampreys usually live in the ocean—but <u>this destructive species needs</u> to spawn in fresh water. ☐28

25. A. NO CHANGE
    B. *Petromyzon marinus* the sea, lamprey
    C. *Petromyzon marinus*, the sea lamprey
    D. *Petromyzon marinus* the sea lamprey

26. F. NO CHANGE
    G. lamprey's impact is
    H. lampreys' impact is
    J. lamprey's impact are

27. A. NO CHANGE
    B. this destructive species need
    C. this destructive specie needs
    D. this destructive specie's needs

28. Which of the following sequences of sentences will make Paragraph 1 flow most logically?
    F. NO CHANGE
    G. 1, 4, 2, 3
    H. 3, 1, 4, 2
    J. 2, 1, 4, 3

[2]

Ever since these aggressive creatures invaded, the Great Lakes, by way of the St. Lawrence Seaway, and interlake canals, they have been a problem. The eel-like lamprey feeds on other fish by latching onto an unsuspecting victim with its teeth-ringed sucker mouth. The teeth and the long, bony, raspy tongue grind through the skin of the fish. To reach the blood and body tissues. A lamprey will often feed relentlessly until the host dies. These aquatic vampires have an appetite for trout, catfish, salmon, and other game fish.

[3]

In the 1930s, the annual trout catch was millions of pounds; by 1950, the catch was almost zero. Something needed to be done before this parasitic invader wiped out all the game fish in the Great Lakes. 31

29. A. NO CHANGE
B. Ever since these aggressive creatures invaded the Great Lakes, by way of the St. Lawrence Seaway and interlake canals,
C. Ever since these aggressive creatures invaded the Great Lakes by way of the St. Lawrence Seaway and interlake canals,
D. Ever since, these aggressive creatures invaded the Great Lakes by way of the St. Lawrence Seaway and interlake canals,

30. F. NO CHANGE
G. the skin of the fish, to reach the blood
H. the skin of the fish to reach the blood
J. the skin of the fish; to reach the blood

31. The author wants to add this sentence after the topic sentence in Paragraph 3:

With no natural predators, the lamprey population was killing off the native fish species.

Is this a suitable addition to the passage?

A. Yes, because it gives a relevant emphasis as to why the trout supply was dwindling.
B. No, because it does not give pertinent information that supports the paragraph.
C. Yes, because it provides a positive description of the lamprey population.
D. No, because it is redundant and provides no rhetorical purpose to the passage.

[4]

Both the United States and the Canadian governments teamed up to tackle the problem using lamprey-proof water barriers and pesticides that are specific to lampreys. In
32
one ambitious program, sterilized male lampreys have been released back into the lakes to breed with females, whom then lay
33
infertile eggs. Scientists are even trying to crack the lamprey's genetic code in hopes of finding a weak spot.

[5]

Nevertheless, these efforts are showing
34
results—the native fish populations are rebounding as the lampreys decline in numbers. However, the cost of lamprey eradication is dear; currently a yearly budget
35
of almost thirty million dollars is being spent to control this problem. Only vigilance that is
36
constant and watchful will keep the sea
37
lamprey from once again taking over the Great Lakes.

32. F. NO CHANGE
G. lamprey-specific pesticides
H. specific pesticides for lampreys
J. pesticides that are lamprey specific

33. A. NO CHANGE
B. females, whom then lay, infertile eggs
C. females, which then lay infertile eggs
D. females who then lay, infertile eggs

34. F. NO CHANGE
G. Hence
H. Then
J. Conversely

35. A. NO CHANGE
B. is dear: currently; a yearly budget
C. is dear, currently, a yearly budget
D. is dear; currently, a yearly budget

36. F. NO CHANGE
G. constantly watchful vigilance
H. constant, watchful, vigilance
J. constant vigilance

37. A. NO CHANGE
B. keep
C. were kept
D. will be keeping

Rin Tin Tin, Canine Star

[1]

The roster of talented animals from the days <u>of silent film with no talking</u> reads like a
₃₈
circus parade: Anna May the Elephant, Jackie the MGM Lion, Joe Martin the Orangutan, Susie the Chicken … the list goes on and on. <u>But one animal star above the rest stood head</u>
₃₉
<u>and furry shoulders.</u> His name was Rin Tin Tin.

[2]

Lee Duncan discovered Rin Tin Tin under desperate circumstances. In France during World War I, Duncan chanced upon a bombed-out German war-dog kennel. In the <u>rubble he found: a small</u> German shepherd
₄₀
pup still alive. <u>Duncan himself an orphan, felt</u>
₄₁
<u>pity for the poor lost animal,</u> so he slipped the warm bundle inside his uniform jacket and took the pup with him—all the way back to the States.

38. F. NO CHANGE
    G. of no-talking silent film
    H. of silent film
    J. of silent-talking film

39. A. NO CHANGE
    B. But one animal star stood head and furry shoulders above the rest.
    C. But above the rest stood one animal star's head and furry shoulders.
    D. But one animal star stood head above the rest and furry shoulders.

40. F. NO CHANGE
    G. rubble, he found: a small
    H. rubble he found, a small
    J. rubble, he found a small

41. A. NO CHANGE
    B. Duncan, himself an orphan, felt pity for the poor, lost animal,
    C. Duncan, himself an orphan felt pity for the poor, lost animal,
    D. Duncan himself an orphan felt pity for the poor lost animal

Diagnostic Test

[3]

Duncan named the dog Rin Tin Tin after a French good-luck doll. Rinty, as Duncan nicknamed him, was bright and alert, and <u>it</u> easily learned tricks. At a dog show, a photographer trying out his new slow-motion camera used Rinty as a model. He filmed Duncan's dog bounding over an eleven-foot barricade as if it were nothing—and Rinty did it with energy and personality too. When the photographer <u>selled</u> his film to a movie company, Duncan thought Rinty might have a future in film.

[4]

<u>Incidentally,</u> moviegoers loved animal films. Enthusiastic fans followed the careers of animal stars as much as those of human actors. Trained animals were perfect for silent film, since voice commands would not be heard as the trainer coached the animal actor through a scene. Trainers give animals treats for a job well done. When Rin Tin Tin got his paw in the door, moviegoers immediately loved <u>them</u>. [46]

42. F. NO CHANGE
    G. Duncan
    H. he
    J. the doll

43. A. NO CHANGE
    B. sold
    C. sells
    D. sell

44. F. NO CHANGE
    G. Unfortunately
    H. However
    J. Instead

45. A. NO CHANGE
    B. him
    C. you
    D. me

46. Which sentence in Paragraph 4 disturbs the flow and should be deleted?
    F. NO CHANGE
    G. Enthusiastic fans followed the careers of animal stars as much as those of human actors.
    H. Trainers give animals treats for a job well done.
    J. When Rin Tin Tin got his paw in the door, moviegoers immediately loved him.

Diagnostic Test

[5]

[1] When Rin Tin Tin <u>died in 1932, radio broadcasts are interrupted</u> with the sad news, and his fans were <u>dejected</u>. [2] Rin Tin Tin appeared in twenty-three films, sometimes even playing a wolf! [3] Reportedly, the last film Anne Frank got to see before going into hiding was a Rin Tin Tin adventure. [4] His films appeared worldwide. 49

47. A. NO CHANGE
B. died in 1932, radio broadcasts were interrupted
C. dies in 1932, radio broadcasts were interrupted
D. die in 1932, radio broadcasts is interrupted

48. F. NO CHANGE
G. despairing
H. heartbroken
J. forlorn

49. Which of the following sequences of sentences will make Paragraph 5 flow most logically?
A. NO CHANGE
B. 4, 3, 1, 2
C. 3, 1, 2, 4
D. 2, 4, 3, 1

Question 50 asks about the preceding passage as a whole.

50. Suppose the writer wanted to add the following sentence as a conclusion to the essay:

Rin Tin Tin's star still adorns Hollywood's Walk of Fame.

Would this be a good addition to the passage?

F. Yes, because it shows the iconic fame Rin Tin Tin has achieved.
G. No, because it switches the focus from Rin Tin Tin to Hollywood.
H. Yes, because it gives readers a reason to visit Rin Tin Tin's star.
J. No, because it offers no relevant information for the passage.

13

DIAGNOSTIC TEST EVALUATION CHART

Use the chart below to better focus your study as you prepare for the PLAN English Test. Identify the questions you answered incorrectly. Turn to the appropriate chapters, read the explanations, and complete the extra exercises. Review other chapters as needed. Finally, complete the practice tests as final preparation for the PLAN English Test.

**Note that some questions appear in more than one chapter, indicating an overlap in skills needed to answer the question.

Chapter	Question Number
Chapter 2: Topic, Purpose, and Focus	10, 19, 23, 31, 46
Chapter 3: Organization, Unity, and Coherence	12, 20, 24, 28, 34, 44, 49, 50
Chapter 4: Word Choice	7, 11, 15, 16, 22, 32, 36, 38, 42, 48
Chapter 5: Sentence Structure	4, 5, 6, 17, 30, 33, 37, 39, 47
Chapter 6: Usage	1, 3, 13, 18, 27, 31, 43, 45
Chapter 7: Punctuation	2, 8, 9, 14, 21, 25, 26, 29, 35, 40, 41

Chapter 1
Preparing for the PLAN English Test

THE PLAN ENGLISH TEST

This book focuses on the **English Test** portion of the PLAN. When you take the PLAN, you will be given 30 minutes to answer 50 questions in the English Test section. The following two categories and six elements of effective writing are included in the English Test:

Usage/Mechanics

- punctuation
- grammar and usage
- sentence structure

Rhetorical Skills

- strategy
- organization
- style

The chapters in this book focus on reviewing specific skills. The chapters do not teach these skills, which you have spent time learning throughout your education, but they offer examples and help you to practice specifically what you will be tested on in the PLAN. The questions used in the exercises throughout the chapters and in the review at the end of each chapter are very similar in wording and focus to actual questions you will see on the PLAN.

The Diagnostic Test at the beginning of the book and two Practice Tests at the end are simulated PLAN English tests. They are the same length and contain passages and questions comparable to those you will see on the PLAN English Test. Review your scores on these practice tests with your teacher or tutor to determine if there are skill areas you need to hone before taking the PLAN.

For practice with other sections of the PLAN, refer to these titles from American Book Company:

PLAN Mathematics Test Preparation Guide

PLAN Reading Test Preparation Guide

PLAN Science Test Preparation Guide

Preparing for the PLAN English Test

FREQUENTLY ASKED QUESTIONS

What is the PLAN?

The PLAN is a test that helps tenth graders measure academic progress at the midpoint of their high school careers. Whether you are a college-bound student or planning to enter the workforce after high school, PLAN results can help you assess where you are and what skills you might need to improve.

How long is the exam?

The full PLAN includes 145 multiple-choice questions and takes approximately one hour and fifty-five minutes to complete. The exam has four sections: English, math, reading, and science.

When can I take PLAN?

The PLAN is taken in your tenth grade year. Your school administrator or guidance counselor will announce the exact times, dates, and places for the test.

How do I sign up?

Your counselor should have details about PLAN registration and fees.

What should I bring on test day?

- your school ID number or Social Security number to identify your PLAN record
- three sharpened soft-lead (No. 2) pencils with good erasers
- a watch to pace yourself (no beepers, please)
- a calculator for the math test (optional)

Should I guess an answer?

Just as on the ACT, there is no penalty for guessing an answer. Be sure to answer every question.

Read all the possible answers before choosing one. Eliminate every answer you know is wrong. Then pick the best one from those left.

For more details about the PLAN, please visit ACT, Inc. at http://www.actstudent.org/plan/.

Chapter 1

Tips for PLAN Preparation and Testing

The PLAN measures your overall learning, so if you have paid attention throughout your schooling, you should do well! It would be difficult, if not impossible, to "cram" for an exam as comprehensive as this. However, you can study wisely by using a PLAN-specific guide (like this book) for practice in answering the same types of questions that will be asked on the PLAN (included in this book; additional practice tests are available online from PLAN, Inc.).

Preparing for the PLAN

- Believe in yourself! Attitude plays a big part in how well you do anything. Keep your thoughts positive. Tell yourself you will do well on the exam.
- Be prepared. Get a good eight hours of sleep the night before your exam. Eat a well-balanced meal, one that contains plenty of proteins and carbohydrates, prior to your exam.
- Arrive early. Allow yourself at least 15–20 minutes to find your room and get settled. Then you can relax before the exam, so you won't feel rushed.
- Practice relaxation techniques. Some students become overly worried about exams. Before or during the test, they may perspire heavily, experience an upset stomach, or have shortness of breath. If you feel any of these symptoms, talk to a close friend or see a counselor. They will suggest ways to deal with test anxiety. Here are some quick ways to relieve test anxiety:
    - Imagine yourself in your favorite place. Let yourself sit there and relax.
    - Do a body scan. Tense and relax each part of your body starting with your toes and ending with your forehead.
    - Use the 3-12-6 method of relaxation when you feel stress. Inhale slowly for 3 seconds. Hold your breath for 12 seconds, and then exhale slowly for 6 seconds.

Taking the PLAN

- Carefully **read the instructions** on the PLAN test booklet.
- Once you are told that you may open the booklet, **read the directions for each test** thoroughly before beginning to mark answers.
- **Read each question carefully**, and use your best approach for answering the questions. Some test-takers like to skim the questions and answers before reading the problem or passage. Others prefer to work the problem or read the passage before looking at the answers. Decide which approach works best for you.
- **Answer each question** on the exam, as your score is based on the number of questions answered correctly. There is no penalty for guessing, but every spot left blank is automatically graded as a zero.

Preparing for the PLAN English Test

- If you are uncertain about an answer, **take an educated guess**. Eliminate choices that are definitely wrong, and then choose from the remaining answers.

- **Use your answer sheet correctly**. Make sure the number on your question matches the number on your answer sheet. If you need to change your answer, erase your original answer completely. Use a No. 2 pencil to write, and make sure the answers are dark. The computerized scanner may be unable to read answers that are too light.

- **Check your answers**. If you finish a test before time is called, review your exam to make sure you have chosen the best responses. Change answers only if you are sure they are wrong.

- Be sure to **pace yourself**. Since you will have a limited amount of time, be careful not to spend too much time on one passage or problem, leaving you no time to complete the rest of the test. Listen for the announcement of five minutes remaining on each test.

- When time is called for each test, **put your pencil down**. If you continue to write or erase after time has been called, you run the risk of being dismissed and your test being disqualified from scoring.

WHAT TO LOOK FOR WHEN YOU TAKE THE PLAN ENGLISH TEST

- The PLAN English Test is comprised of **four essays** (or passages), each of which have underlined and numbered sections of text. The column next to the passages contains questions with corresponding numbers.

- Note the **style** and **structure** of each passage, including word choice, tone, and so on. Pay attention to what **rhetorical devices** or **elements of writing** are used in the underlined parts of the passage. Think about the **purpose** and **focus** of each passage.

- Regardless of the fact that only portions of a passage are underlined, be sure to **skim the whole passage**. Some questions ask about a section of the passage, but some ask about the passage as a whole.

- **Read the answer choices carefully**. Although there are no "trick questions" on the PLAN, there may be subtle differences in answers. If two answers seem to make sense to you, read them again, determine how they differ, and decide which one *best* answers the question.

- When answering a question about an underlined part of a passage, **reread the sentence, substituting your selected answer**. Decide if it makes sense and, if it does not, reconsider the other answers.

- Remember that you will not be tested on rote recall of grammar rules, spelling, or vocabulary. Instead, you will be tested on your understanding of written Standard English (punctuation, grammar, usage, and sentence structure) and rhetorical skills (strategy, organization, and style).

Chapter 1

How the PLAN English Test Will Look

On the PLAN, **Usage/Mechanics** questions refer to an underlined word or phrase in the essay. When you answer these questions, you need to make the best choice of words or punctuation for the underlined section. **Rhetorical Skills** questions can ask about underlined portions as well, or they may be about a paragraph, section, or about the entire essay. Be aware that some questions may also directly or indirectly address more than one skill in Usage/Mechanics (**UM**) and Rhetorical Skills (**RS**). Most questions include the option of choosing NO CHANGE as your answer; if the selection is best left as it is written, then this is the answer you should choose.

Read the following excerpt from a passage; then, on your own, try answering the questions that follow. After you answer them, study the explanations about which answer is the correct one and why.

Sample Passage

Directions: Some portions in the following passage have been underlined and numbered. The matching questions in the right-hand column offer alternatives for the underlined portion. You can choose one of these, or select NO CHANGE if the original version in the passage is best. If a number appears in a box within the text, the corresponding question will ask about a section of the text that is not underlined (such as a whole paragraph). To choose the best answer for any question, you should read more than just the underlined portion.

How Candlemas Became Groundhog Day

[1]

What do candles and groundhogs have in common? They share <u>a holiday or rather a holy day</u>.
                                    1

Sample Questions and Explanations

1. **A.** NO CHANGE
   B. a holiday, or rather a holy day
   C. a holiday, or rather, a holy day
   D. a holiday or rather, a holy day

Which answer did you choose? This is a punctuation question (UM). To answer it correctly, you need to remember the rules for using commas with parenthetical statements. The correct answer is C, because the phrase "or rather" is a parenthetical statement that is not necessary to the sentences and, therefore, is set off by commas.

For Christians, this holy day <u>began</u> in the
                                        2
in the fourth century, but it has even older

roots in Judaism. Mosaic Law said <u>a new

baby boy's mother</u> must be purified at the
                3
temple forty days after the birth. December 25

was set as Jesus' birth. Forty days later, Mary

<u>would have traveled to go to</u> the temple for
            4
purification. It lasts three days, starting on

February 2. The Catholic Church has always

celebrated the day with processions and the

blessing of candles for the year: Candlemas.

2. **F.** NO CHANGE
   G. begins
   H. begun
   J. beginning

This is a sentence structure question (UM) that focuses on correct verb tense. To answer it correctly, you need to skim the text as a whole and see that it is written in the past tense. You also must consider the context and choose the verb that fits the sentence. The correct answer is F, NO CHANGE, because "began" is the correct verb tense to use here.

3. **A.** NO CHANGE
   B. the new mother of a baby boy
   C. a baby boy's mother that's new
   D. the new mother with her baby boy

This is an organization question (RS), focusing on the order and coherence of ideas. To answer it correctly, think about the most logical, least awkward way to express the idea here. The point made in the passage is that a woman who has a baby is a new mother; if she has a baby boy, she should be purified after the birth. The clearest way to express this is B.

4. **F.** NO CHANGE
   G. would traveled
   H. would have gone to
   J. would be going to

This is a sentence structure question focusing on correct verb use (UM). The correct answer is H, because it is a simple and correct (in verb form and tense) replacement for wordy and redundant language in the original text.

Chapter 1

[2]

The connection with groundhogs comes from Europe. Long ago, they came up with weather-predicting rhymes for February 2, Candlemas Day. All the rhymes predicted that if clear weather dawned on Candlemas Day, their would be more winter weather before spring. Historically, Germans thought of looking for an animal's shadow on that day for a prediction.

5. **A.** NO CHANGE
   B. it
   C. groundhogs
   D. Europeans

This is a word choice question (RS) about pronoun use. The existing pronoun, "they," has no antecedent in the context—unless it could refer to groundhogs, which is unlikely! Thus, C is not correct either. Answer B is not correct, because it substitutes one unclear pronoun for another. The correct answer is D, because it clearly states who created the rhymes.

6. **F.** NO CHANGE
   G. there would be more winter weather
   H. their would be more winter whether
   J. there would be more winter whether

This is a usage question (UM) dealing with commonly confused word pairs. The pairs in question are "their/there" and "weather/whether." The only answer that features the correct word from each pair is G.

21

Preparing for the PLAN English Test

The Germans thought hedgehogs were wise and would know if they had to return to their dens for more <u>winter. So, the Germans watched</u> the furry creatures on February 2.
                                                 7

[3]

Europeans immigrating to America saw the groundhog as the closest relative to the hedgehog. The Europeans wanted to keep their traditions and chose the groundhog as their new weather expert. Groundhogs are rodents like big squirrels, while hedgehogs are spiny mammals. On February 2, people still watch groundhogs to keep themselves enlightened about spring's arrival. [8]

7. What is the best way to combine these two sentences?
   A. winter; so the Germans watched
   B. winter, so the Germans watched
   C. winter so, they watched
   D. winter, so they watched

This is a sentence structure question (UM) involving joining two sentences. The correct answer is D, because two independent clauses can be joined by a comma plus a conjunction ("so"). When a semicolon joins two sentences, no conjunction is used, so the answer is not A. The comma comes before the conjunction, so the answer cannot be C. The other aspect of the question involves changing "the Germans" to "they" to avoid repetition; thus, while punctuated correctly, B is not correct.

8. Which sentence in paragraph 3 is irrelevant and could be eliminated?
   F. Europeans immigrating to America saw the groundhog as the closest relative to the hedgehog.
   G. The Europeans wanted to keep their traditions and chose the groundhog as their new weather expert.
   H. Groundhogs are rodents like big squirrels, while hedgehogs are spiny mammals.
   J. On February 2, people still watch groundhogs to keep them enlightened about spring's arrival.

This is a topic development question (RS) that requires you to choose the sentence which is irrelevant to the overall paragraph. The best answer is H, as this sentence provides extra information that is unnecessary. It is the only sentence that can be taken out without disrupting the flow and clarity of the paragraph.

Chapter 1

GOING FORWARD

Read the chapters in this book for more tips and examples of various questions that you will see on the PLAN English Test. Best of all, each chapter review will give you plenty of realistic PLAN English Test questions to practice answering. Of course, don't forget about the Diagnostic Test at the beginning of the book and the two Practice Tests at the end, each of which simulates a full PLAN English Test.

Chapter 2
Topic, Purpose, and Focus

Topic, purpose, and focus questions on the PLAN English Test earn points in the following way, ranging from fundamental skills in identifying focus (up to 19 score points) to sophisticated skills in topic development (28–32 points):

Points	Benchmark Description
13–15	
16–19	Identify the basic purpose or role of a specified phrase or sentence Delete a clause or sentence because it is obviously irrelevant to the essay
20–23	Identify the central idea or main topic of a straightforward piece of writing Determine relevancy when presented with a variety of sentence-level details
24–27	Identify the focus of a simple essay, applying that knowledge to add a sentence that sharpens that focus or to determine if an essay has met a specified goal Delete material primarily because it disturbs the flow and development of the paragraph Add a sentence to accomplish a fairly straightforward purpose such as illustrating a given statement
28–32	Apply an awareness of the focus and purpose of a fairly involved essay to determine the rhetorical effect and suitability of an existing phrase or sentence, or to determine the need to delete plausible but irrelevant material Add a sentence to accomplish a subtle rhetorical purpose such as to emphasize, to add supporting detail, or to express meaning through connotation

On the PLAN English Test, you will be tested on standards for college readiness. As stated in chapter 1, you can find each standard and its explanation on the PLAN website (http://www.actstudent.org/plan/). The next few chapters will go into more detail about each standard.

Some questions might ask you to identify the focus of essays and determine how well those essays fulfill their purpose with supporting details. In some cases, you may have to delete clauses or sentences that are irrelevant to the main focus of a passage or that disrupt its flow. When you understand the central topic of a piece of writing and recognize the author's purpose, it becomes easier to identify material that does or does not serve a useful rhetorical purpose (e.g., emphasizing a point, adding detail, using connotations to express meaning).

Focus

Focus means directing your attention toward a particular point and seeing it clearly. Without focus, nothing stands out, and nothing can be seen for what it is (or identified as being). Let's consider focus as it relates to a telescope. A telescope is typically used for seeing objects that are far away. To do so, it uses magnification and focus. The telescope can magnify, but if it is not focused, it becomes almost useless. Without focus, a telescope's purpose of allowing a person to see something more clearly is never achieved.

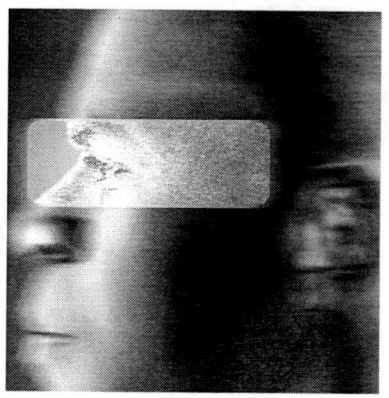

Focus is just as important for **topic development** in writing. Through writing, you may direct your audience's attention toward an idea, but without focus they will not see your point with clarity. And having your audience see your point clearly is the purpose of any writing.

Let's look more closely at the focus used by the telescope. If you want to look at the full moon, you can go outside on the right night and look up into the sky. Depending on cloud conditions and city lights, you can probably get a pretty good idea of what the moon looks like. You may see light and dark spots on the lunar surface. And if you use a little imagination, you may even see a pattern that looks like "the man in the moon."

Without a telescope, though, your focus is very limited. Looking up at the sky, it is sometimes difficult to focus just on the moon. The moon is big, but it's very far away and surrounded by lots of space and stars. There may be some other distractions, like the blinking lights of passing airplanes or a veil of floating clouds. All of these distractions make it hard to really focus on the moon itself.

The same principles hold true with writing. As you read written pieces, you may come across words, phrases, or sentences that distract you from the central idea. Details that have nothing to do with the main topic of a text—like those drifting clouds or blinking airplane lights in the moon example—should be revised or taken out. When you take a careful look at the central topic of a passage, you should realize that there are plenty of details that *do* support and enhance the text.

Focused Main Idea

You have written many essays in response to writing prompts given by your teacher, so you understand the importance of focusing on the main idea. For an essay to have a real impact on the audience, it must have a focused main topic with a point that can be seen clearly. The writer then maintains the focus throughout the **supporting details** of each paragraph so that they stay related to the **central idea**. This support may include assumptions, reasoning, emotion, irony, humor, examples, testimony, or data, but it should be specific, not general.

Chapter 2

One common mistake many writers make is retreating from the subject matter of an essay as they gather details to support it. You may have run into this problem yourself when you tried to organize your response to a writing prompt. It's helpful to brainstorm and jot down ideas that relate to the main focus; just don't stray too far off track. If an essay is about the meaning of ambition, it shouldn't focus too much on being competitive or about creating a positive self-image. If it's about illiteracy, it shouldn't delve too deeply into faulty school reading programs. By establishing a clearly focused main idea from the beginning, you are able to more easily determine which details would effectively support that main idea.

Here are two example paragraphs, both written to address the main idea, which addresses the causes of poverty. Which paragraph is focused and supported by details? Which one has details that may actually distract from the main idea, even to the point that it's hard to tell what the main idea is?

Example 1:

Did you know that if you put together the wealth of the three richest people in the world, you would have more than if you combined the production of goods and services of the world's 48 poorest countries? One of the reasons for this is that trade between nations is not often based on equal exchange. There is also enough food for everyone in the world to have more than what they need. The fact that democracy is not practiced in every country could be a major factor too. Poverty is the most important social issue that should be addressed because it affects every other area of life: food, education, medical care, human rights, and others. We can make a change.

Example 2:

Poverty is a complex social issue, and there are many theories that attempt to explain its causes. One theory is that poverty can be explained by the circumstances in which poor individuals find themselves. For example, most poor individuals do not have adequate education. They may also lack the opportunities to obtain jobs that can produce livable incomes. Other seemingly indirect factors, like ill health or discrimination, can also play a major role in an individual's staying poor. There is no simple explanation for the causes of poverty, but looking closely at how just one poor person lives, may help us to find some answers.

If you thought the first example paragraph was hard to follow, that's because it drifts away from the subject matter too often with distracting and disorganized details. The writer gets caught up in discussing the uneven trade between nations, the world's food supply, and the government systems of different countries. These factors may relate to poverty, but the author doesn't focus on the *causes* of poverty. The second paragraph is focused specifically on the factors that cause poverty and gives concrete examples: inadequate education, lack of opportunities, poor health, and so on.

Topic, Purpose, and Focus

Remember, you might be asked to add or delete material from a certain passage. Determine if it is a **relevant detail** based on the focus and purpose of the passage. Then make your decision on the best answer.

Now read the following passage, and answer questions about its focus.

"If only there were more hours in the day" is a statement that I have made both outwardly and inwardly, but would one more hour really make a difference? I would like to think that it would; however, I know that I could easily fill that additional hour with other projects and chores until I felt, once again, that I needed just one more hour. Life is a series of complications without end. Just take a look at the schedule of any mother in America today, and you will see a hectic day of chores, lessons, and other obligations that is full from sunup to well past sundown. But I think that it is really a matter of perspective and priority. In order to live a life of simplicity, I have to make time for the simple things in life and just not worry about all the rest. This means cooking one less meal so that I can spend time with someone I love, or running one less errand on Saturday so that I can have a picnic with my family. So the problem is whether I really need that hour, or just a different outlook on life.

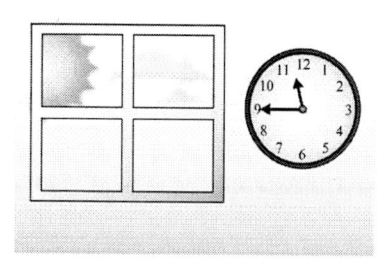

1. What is the central idea the writer is trying to express?

   A. There should be extra hours in the day so we can get more important things done.

   B. American mothers have too many chores to complete each day.

   C. A simple life isn't as fulfilling as one filled with lots of activities.

   D. We should prioritize our duties and take time to appreciate the simple pleasures of life.

The correct answer is D. The author focuses on the problem of having a hectic lifestyle and decides it's better to readjust one's outlook on life than to scramble to get everything done in the limited hours of the day.

Chapter 2

2. What sentence should you add after the underlined sentence to further emphasize its message?

F. That's not to say that cooking and running errands aren't important.

G. After all, those chores will still be there the next day; the chance to be with loved ones may not.

H. Just remember that your family could be mad if you don't have dinner ready for them.

J. It's okay to shirk your duties and fritter away your life on pleasurable activities.

Answer G is the best choice; it highlights the idea that we should consider what's most important in life. The other choices negate that message.

Practice 1: Focus

Directions: Some portions in the following passage have been underlined and numbered. The matching questions offer alternatives for the underlined portion. You can choose one of these, or select NO CHANGE if the original version in the passage is best. If a number appears in a box within the text, the corresponding question will ask about a section of the text that is not underlined (such as a whole paragraph). To choose the best answer for any question, you should read more than just the underlined portion.

The Necessity of Rules

[1]

A hungry eleven-year-old hops behind the wheel of a vacant taxi to drive himself a few blocks to the ice cream shop. Barely able to see over the wheel, he runs over two trashcans and a fire hydrant on the way. He meets two young friends at the shop, one who had driven on the wrong side of the street the whole way and the other who had crashed into a parked car and a street sweeper as he veered along. The police and the boys' parents do nothing in response.

[2]

A woman decides that she wants a bigger TV, so she walks downstairs to her neighbor's apartment and takes his. The neighbor objects, and the woman punches him and continues on her way with the TV. No police come, and the woman never goes to jail. [1]

Topic, Purpose, and Focus

[3]

Events like the ones above would be common, everyday occurrences in a society without rules. In such a society, people could do what they wanted, when they wanted to, and they would answer to no one. At first, this might sound very appealing. Don't feel like going to school? Stay home and sleep in! Want your classmate's new jacket? Take it! Life could be easy and stress-free with no rules. But, consider the fact that no one else would be following rules either. <u>If someone liked the new sneakers you saved for all summer, that person could take them, and you would have to wait for a sale at the store to buy new ones if you didn't have enough money.</u>[2] If a pharmacist decided she didn't want to go to work anymore, your grandfather might not be able to get his heart medication. If the train conductors and bus drivers felt like staying home, people who relied on those modes of transportation to get to their own jobs might become unemployed. Everyone else would be enjoying the same freedoms that you would and, at least some of the time, it would be at your expense.

[4]

While we may not always like following rules, rules serve an important function. Knowing that there are rules that govern our behavior keeps people accountable for their actions, especially when people are punished for breaking those rules. Rules also keep people safe, both from themselves and from others. There is a reason that eleven-year-olds are not allowed to drive, just as there is a reason that killing someone is against the law. <u>Imagine the fear and chaos in a society where actions like stealing and killing were commonplace and not punishable.</u>[3] Every functioning society needs a set of rules that everyone knows and follows, with enforcement of those rules in the form of police and the rest of the justice system.

[5]

Rules are important for a group to maintain order and productivity. People in a society depend upon one another, and rules help the different parts of a society interact successfully by giving everyone a common ground. Rules keep everyone in a society feeling safe and secure.[4]

Chapter 2

1. The author wants to delete the first two paragraphs. Based on the focus of this passage, should he make the revision?

   A. No, because they provide vivid examples of scenarios in a world with no rules.

   B. Yes, because they make negative assumptions about people who follow their desires.

   C. Yes, because they show that the police are ineffectual at stopping crime.

   D. No, because they imagine a frightening vision of the future.

2. F. NO CHANGE

   G. If someone liked the new sneakers you saved for all summer, that person could take them, even if they looked better on you.

   H. If someone liked the new sneakers you saved for all summer, that person could take them from you.

   J. If someone liked the new sneakers you saved for all summer, that person could take them away one at a time or even both at once.

3. What sentence should you add after the underlined sentence in Paragraph 4 to sharpen its focus?

   A. Rules are in place to protect people's belongings, health, and safety.

   B. Life would be like the video game *Grand Theft Auto* or the novel *Lord of the Flies*.

   C. As long as you were not the one being robbed, such a world could be tolerable.

   D. Rules are needed because a few people ruin a good thing for everyone else.

4. What is the main topic of this passage?

   F. It would be great if you could break the rules when it suits you.

   G. It's bothersome when other people break the rules, and it affects you.

   H. Rules are made to be broken.

   J. Rules ensure that everyone stays safe, and order is maintained.

Topic, Purpose, and Focus

PURPOSE

How do you recognize the **author's purpose**? Ask yourself *why* the author is writing about a particular subject. Every author writes for different reasons. Think of the reasons why you write: you write essays for English class because the teacher requires it; you may write a note in a birthday card to your mother to express your love; or you may send e-mails to Internet friends just to say hello. Every author writes for a specific purpose and a particular **audience**. Often the author's purpose is revealed in the way the author writes, in the way the author chooses words or phrases for their specific meanings. For example, a piece of text may be instructive, descriptive, conversational, or humorous, depending on the author's intent. See if you can determine the purpose in the following two paragraphs.

Example 1

There is much confusion as to whether an animal has antlers or horns. It's really quite simple. If the animal sheds its headgear each year, then it is shedding its antlers. If the animal does not shed its headgear each year, then it possesses horns. Whitetail deer, mule deer, elk, moose and caribou are all members of the deer family and shed their antlers each year. Texas longhorn steers, bulls, water buffalo, bighorn sheep, and bison keep their headgear year-round; therefore, their bony protuberances are horns.

Example 2

A young anthropologist went deer hunting with a grizzled old hunter who had taken many deer. It wasn't long before the old hunter had bagged a buck.

When both men gathered over the downed animal, the old hunter said: "Look at those horns, would you! He's a big ten-pointer!"

"Actually, those are antlers," the young man replied.

"Antlers, horns, what's the difference?" the old hunter said.

"The difference is that if they shed them, they're antlers, not horns," the young man explained.

"So—I've been deer hunting for over forty years and mistakenly calling antlers horns?" the old man asked.

"It seems so, doesn't it?" the young man replied with a smile.

Both paragraphs discuss the difference between antlers and horns, but they do so in different ways. Example 1 presents basic explanatory information about animals that have antlers or horns and enlightens the reader on the difference between the two. Though the paragraphs contain the necessary descriptive words, there is no dialogue or action. This purpose of this paragraph is **to inform**, and it would fit well in a science textbook. So the audience is most likely students or teachers.

Example 2, however, describes characters and their interactions using dialogue. Instead of educating the reader on the difference between antlers and horns, the author is telling a story. The purpose of this paragraph is **to entertain** a general audience.

Examples 1 and 2 show how an author can use a different **voice** for writing, depending on his or her purpose. That is, the author's choice of words reflects a certain feeling or direction. The purpose is reflected also in the audience for whom the writing is intended. Generally, a writer who is trying to inform or instruct an audience uses a **formal voice**, which includes complex sentence structure and a higher level of vocabulary. An **informal voice** including simple vocabulary, simple sentence structure, and loose following of grammatical rules is acceptable when you're addressing friends or attempting to entertain an audience.

Authors who are clear about their purposes are able to write more effectively because they know the audiences they're writing for and how best to get their messages across to them. The table below identifies several different purposes for writing.

Purpose	Definition	Reading Selection
To inform	To present facts and details	"Ocean Fishes"
To entertain	To amuse or offer enjoyment	"How My Cat Turned Purple"
To persuade	To urge action on an issue	"Raise Penalties for Polluters"
To explain why	To provide clear reasons	"How Plants Grow"
To instruct	To teach concepts and facts	"Mastering Exponents"
To create suspense	To convey uncertainty	"Will Tom Win the Race?"

Topic, Purpose, and Focus

Purpose	Definition	Reading Selection
To motivate	To inspire to act	"You Can Make a Difference!"
To cause doubt	To be skeptical	"Are Adults Responsible?"
To introduce a character	To describe a person's traits	"First Look at Captain Nemo"
To create a mood	To establish atmosphere	"Gloom in the House of Usher"
To relate an adventure	To tell an exciting story	"Lost in a Cave"
To share a personal experience	To tell about an event in your life	"The Time I Learned to Share"
To describe feelings	To communicate emotions through words	"When My Dog Died"

Look at how this is done with the following sample passages. Read each passage, and then answer the question that follows.

In the 1930s, one woman who had lived in a sod home in the 1800s remembered with affection how she could laugh at hard times. Other inhabitants of these homes, however, told quite a different story. During the winter, snow came streaming in through every crevice. It was usually so cold inside the earthen dwelling that people got frostbite even though they would be sitting by a stove wrapped in a quilt. The floors were no more than compacted earth, and if straw was brought in to cover them, it became a breeding ground for fleas. Mice and rats burrowed into the walls and were so ubiquitous that settlers constantly had to kick them out of the way.

1. What do you think the author's purpose is for writing this piece?
   A. To persuade
   B. To inform
   C. To motivate
   D. To entertain

The correct answer is B. The passage describes the living conditions of the 1800s to inform the reader of how difficult it was for people back then. Such a description might appear in a history textbook.

There is a wonderful invention that helps newborns who have medical problems—the new breed of computerized infant incubator bed is here! These beds are incredible in all that they do. They monitor every vital sign you could imagine. In addition to weighing the baby and providing heat in a sterile environment, these incubator beds can accommodate all the necessary medical hookups and even allow the doctor necessary access for performing surgical procedures. As you can guess, these miraculous beds are far from cheap. But you have the opportunity to make a difference in the life of a child by donating your money to help Yellowstone Pediatric Hospital buy more of these necessary and lifesaving beds. Be a miracle maker! Donate your money to Yellowstone today!

2. What do you think the author's purpose is for writing this piece?

   F. To describe an event
   G. To cause doubt
   H. To persuade
   J. To instruct

Answer H is correct. The author of this passage clearly wants to persuade readers to donate money to a hospital so it can buy these high-tech beds. Note the imperative sentences at the end of the passage ("Be a miracle maker! Donate your money to Yellowstone today!") that urge you to support a cause. This type of passage might appear in a hospital's promotional material.

When you understand the purpose of a passage, you can better determine whether a sentence is relevant and strengthens the essay, or whether it's irrelevant and disturbs the flow and development of the passage.

In the previous example, the author wants to add this sentence to the passage:

> Incubators for ill or premature infants were developed in the mid-nineteenth century and modeled after the kind used for chicken eggs.

3. Should the author make this addition?

   A. Yes, because it provides background information on the history of incubators.

   B. No, because infants and chicken eggs are two very different things.

   C. Yes, because it's important to give credit to the scientific minds who invented the infant incubator.

   D. No, because it distracts from the basic purpose, which is to convince people to make donations.

Topic, Purpose, and Focus

The correct answer is D. While the sentence provides related information about the history of incubators, it is irrelevant in terms of the passage's intended purpose.

As you read a passage to determine its purpose, also be aware of the possible **connotations** of words. While **denotations** are the dictionary meanings of words, connotations are the emotional associations we make with words. For example, the words *slender* and *skinny* both mean "thin." However, if you called a person *slender*, that compliment might get you a smile in return. On the other hand, calling the same person *skinny* might be offensive. In a similar way, the words *determined* and *stubborn* both refer to persistence and an unwillingness to be moved from a particular position. However, *determined* carries a positive connotation, while *stubborn* is usually considered a negative word. A writer who uses words with negative connotations may come across as critical or judgmental.

Look at the following sample question.

1. In the action movie, the hero <u>scurried</u> away after detonating the villain's bomb.
   A. NO CHANGE   **B.** skittered   **C.** bounded   **D.** flitted

The best answer is C. We expect an action hero to be brave and tough, and the other answers call to mind the actions of timid animals like mice or birds. *Bounded* carries a more positive connotation, giving the sense of confidence or excitement.

Practice 2: Purpose

Directions: Some portions in the following passage have been underlined and numbered. The matching questions offer alternatives for the underlined portion. You can choose one of these, or select NO CHANGE if the original version in the passage is best. If a number appears in a box within the text, the corresponding question will ask about a section of the text that is not underlined (such as a whole paragraph). To choose the best answer for any question, you should read more than just the underlined portion.

Get to Know the Greenhouse Effect

[1]

Over the years, the issue of global warming has become increasingly controversial. Some people think it simply doesn't exist, while others claim that our coastlines will be under water in a matter of years! Before getting into the debate, it is important to know the basic facts about the key concept related to global warming: the greenhouse effect. ☐1

Chapter 2

[2]

[1]The greenhouse effect is not a bad thing in itself. [2]Greenhouse gases naturally exist in the Earth's atmosphere, such as water vapor, carbon dioxide (CO_2), and ozone (O_3). [3]This is called the greenhouse effect because it is similar to how greenhouse windows let light in while keeping heat from escaping, helping plants survive in cooler months. [4]The heat retained from the greenhouse effect is necessary in order for our survival; otherwise, the planet would be sixty degrees colder! [5]Such a temperature would suit the animals in the Arctic, but regular farm animals require external temperatures ranging from 50 to 68 degrees Fahrenheit to maintain homeothermy, or constant internal body temperatures. [2] [3]

[3]

It stands to reason that if there are more greenhouse gases in the atmosphere, then more heat will be trapped, and the Earth's average temperature will rise. According to scientists, the Earth's temperature has risen one degree in the last hundred years. Many of the world's glaciers are melting now, and some scientists think that this is a result of the Earth getting warmer. The sea levels have also risen six to eight inches over the last hundred years, causing many scientists to attribute this to the glaciers melting. <u>As sea levels rise, dangerous tides become higher and wreak crazy havoc on the world's beaches.</u>[4] All of this goes back to the greenhouse gases, which are <u>leaked</u>[5] whenever we drive cars, use electricity, or do anything that requires the use of fossil fuels (e.g., coal and oil). Scientists think that our contribution of greenhouse gases is the cause of the Earth's slowly rising temperature.

1. The author wants to delete Paragraph 1. Based on the focus of the paragraph, should he make that change?
    A. Yes, because it entertains readers with ridiculous theories.
    B. No, because it persuades readers to stop polluting the air and water with toxins.
    C. Yes, because it creates a suspenseful mood.
    D. No, because it explains how the subject of global warming is controversial.

Topic, Purpose, and Focus

2. Which sentence would you add to Paragraph 2 to illustrate the point that greenhouse gases are necessary for the Earth's atmosphere?

   F. Their job is to trap the heat from the sun and keep it in our atmosphere, thus keeping the Earth warm too.

   G. They trap the heat from the sun and keep it in our atmosphere, making our planet dangerously warm.

   H. They naturally appear in our atmosphere, so they must be useful for some reason.

   J. They keep the planet warm by trapping the sun's rays, but these gases should be eradicated.

3. Which sentence would you delete from Paragraph 2, and why?

   A. NO CHANGE

   B. Sentence 1, because you cannot prove the greenhouse effect isn't a bad thing.

   C. Sentence 3, because it's irrelevant how the greenhouse effect got its name.

   D. Sentence 5, because discussing body temperatures of animals veers away from the focus of the article.

4. F. NO CHANGE

   G. As sea levels rise to dangerous levels, tides become frighteningly higher and wreak havoc on the world's beaches.

   H. As sea levels rise, tides become higher and destroy the world's beaches.

   J. As sea levels rise, dangerous tides become higher and devastate our planet's precious beaches.

5. A. NO CHANGE

   B. oozed out

   C. excreted

   D. released

CHAPTER 2 SUMMARY

Focus is an important component of **topic development** in writing, allowing the audience to see the point with clarity.

A writer maintains the focus throughout the **supporting details** of each paragraph so that the writing stays related to the **central idea**. Details that have nothing to do with the main topic of a text should be revised or taken out.

To recognize the **author's purpose**, ask yourself *why* the author is writing about a particular subject, and identify the intended **audience**.

When considering the author's meaning, be aware of the possible **connotations**, or emotional associations, of words as well as the **denotations**, or dictionary meanings, of words.

CHAPTER 2 REVIEW

Directions: Some portions in the following passage have been underlined and numbered. The matching questions in the right-hand column offer alternatives for the underlined portion. You can choose one of these, or select NO CHANGE if the original version in the passage is best. If a number appears in a box within the text, the corresponding question will ask about a section of the text that is not underlined (such as a whole paragraph). To choose the best answer for any question, you should read more than just the underlined portion.

[1]

The Wonder of Pelé

[1]

Soccer, or *futebol*, has produced more controversy than peace throughout the world. The world expects hard knocks and national loyalty from soccer teams and gets it in abundance. In contrast, the United States

1. What is the main focus of the passage?

   A. The United States differs from the rest of the world by not appreciating soccer.

   B. Pelé united fans from many countries in the spirit of goodwill and sportsmanship.

   C. Pelé and Muhammad Ali struggled to be accepted in the United States.

   D. Pelé became a rich and successful man by playing professional soccer in his youth.

expects high scores and easily recognizable heroes from every sport and finds very little of either in soccer. There was a time, however, when the world and the United States had all their expectations met by one man. This man was named Pelé.

[2]

Pelé was born in 1940 in Tres Coracoes, a poor town in Brazil. His ancestors were African slaves. Pelé began playing soccer professionally at the age of fifteen in 1955 and became a star in the world of soccer by 1958. It was in this year that he played in the World Cup finals, scoring two goals for Brazil against Sweden. Pelé was a great athlete, holding the record for the most goals per game scored in a career. [2]

[3]

Pelé's triumphs on the field, however, pale against his record for promoting peace and soccer throughout the world. He spoke with crowds in America in the 1960s, signing autographs for adoring fans despite high tensions between black and white people over the civil rights movement. [3]

2. Which sentence should be added to the end of Paragraph 2?
   F. He was a nice man who always agreed to have his picture taken with young fans.
   G. He never forgot the people from his hometown who made him the man he was.
   H. His teammates were happy for the wins, but perhaps they were jealous of his success.
   J. He is also the only person to have scored goals in three winning World Cup games.

The author wants to add this sentence to the end of Paragraph 3:

   In 1977, Pelé met with boxer Muhammad Ali, who, as a black athlete, had not been wholly accepted by American society during the previous two decades.

3. What is the purpose of this addition?
   A. To show that Muhammad Ali and Pelé were friends and respected one another
   B. To illustrate the point that racial tensions existed during the civil rights movement
   C. To emphasize that boxing wasn't as popular in America as soccer
   D. To explain that Muhammad Ali had been boxing in the United States for twenty years

Chapter 2

[4]

Though popular around the world, including the United States, Pelé stayed loyal to his home country of Brazil until his career ended, <u>spurning</u> offers of millions of dollars
4
from other teams. In his last exhibition game, he played for both teams: one in the first half, the other in the second half. In order to promote soccer in the United States, Pelé signed to play with the New York Cosmos after he retired from the Brazilian team at age thirty-four. The original New York Cosmos team was active from 1971 to 1985, but a new Cosmos team was introduced in 2010. His fame, personality, and ability won millions of United States fans for the sport of soccer. [5]

4. F. NO CHANGE
    G. declining
    H. rejecting
    J. shunning

5. Which sentence in Paragraph 4 should be deleted because it is irrelevant?

    A. In his last exhibition game, he played for both teams: one in the first half, the other in the second half.

    B. Though popular around the world, including the United States, Pelé stayed loyal to his home country of Brazil until his career ended, spurning offers of millions of dollars from other teams.

    C. Pelé signed to play with the New York Cosmos after he retired from the Brazilian team at age thirty-four.

    D. The original New York Cosmos team was active from 1971 to 1985, but a new Cosmos team was introduced in 2010.

[5]

Pelé is now a wealthy man. He still feels the pull of his fans and of the great need for peace around the world. He says that more than wanting children to follow his example on the soccer field, he would like them to follow his example of sportsmanship off the field in the wider world. As a great athlete, Pelé has demonstrated good will and dignity to his legions of fans. That is the wonder of Pelé.

6. **F.** NO CHANGE
   G. mobs
   H. hordes
   J. swarms

Chapter 3
Organization, Unity, and Coherence

Organization and unity questions on the PLAN English Test earn points in the following way, ranging from fundamental skills in organization (up to 15 score points) to sophisticated skills in unity and coherence (28–32 points):

Points	Benchmark Description
13–15	Use conjunctive adverbs or phrases to show time relationships in simple narrative essays (e.g., *then, this time*)
16–19	Select the most logical place to add a sentence in a paragraph
20–23	Use conjunctive adverbs or phrases to express straightforward logical relationships (e.g., *first, afterward, in response*)
	Decide the most logical place to add a sentence in an essay
	Add a sentence that introduces a simple paragraph
24–27	Determine the need for conjunctive adverbs or phrases to create subtle logical connections between sentences (e.g., *therefore, however, in addition*)
	Rearrange the sentences in a fairly uncomplicated paragraph for the sake of logic
	Add a sentence to introduce or conclude the essay or to provide a transition between paragraphs when the essay is fairly straightforward
28–32	Make sophisticated distinctions concerning the logical use of conjunctive adverbs or phrases, particularly when signaling a shift between paragraphs
	Rearrange sentences to improve the logic and coherence of a complex paragraph
	Add a sentence to introduce or conclude a fairly complex paragraph

In this chapter, we will focus more on the rhetorical skills covered on the PLAN English Test. On the test, you might read a passage and then answer questions about revising it. For example, you may be asked how to rearrange sentences into a logical order or whether to add sentences to introduce or conclude the essay. You might even be asked to choose which transitions show a logical relationship to the rest of the passage. In order to answer these questions properly, you will need to review what you have learned about **organization** and **unity**.

43

Organization, Unity, and Coherence

PARAGRAPHS

In the previous chapter, you reviewed how to add sentences to clarify illustrations and how to detect and delete irrelevant details. However, on the PLAN English Test, you might also be required to choose a sentence to properly introduce or conclude a paragraph. In order to do that, you must remember the structure and purpose of a paragraph.

A **paragraph** is a group of sentences that are related. A single main idea unifies each paragraph. Usually, the **introductory sentence**, which appears at the beginning of the paragraph, presents the main idea. The **concluding sentence**, on the other hand, is often a summary of the information in the passage and comes at the end of the paragraph.

Example:

1. The cave's ceiling was covered with jagged stalactites.

2. The cave was a fearsome sight.

3. Bats were flying and squeaking in the cavern.

4. Chet relit the kerosene lantern, bathing the cavern in light.

Logical order for this paragraph: Chet relit the kerosene lantern, bathing the cavern with light. The cave's ceiling was covered with jagged stalactites. Bats were flying and squeaking through the cavern. The cave was a fearsome sight.

Here, Sentence 4 was the introductory sentence, because it explained what the paragraph would describe. Sentence 2 was the concluding sentence, because it provided a summary of the action in the paragraph.

Look at this sample question.

> Nathan and John drove north of Birmingham to go fishing in Wheeler Lake. They stopped at a bait and tackle shop, bought some lures, and drove to the lake. Together, they caught one dozen fish in the lake. [1]

1. Which of the following sentences would best conclude this paragraph?

    A. They always go to Wheeler Lake on Saturdays.

    B. They cleaned the fish at home and had a feast.

    C. John drives the boat, and Nathan baits the lines.

    D. Nathan is a better fisherman than John is.

Answer B is the correct answer. While the other sentences add interesting (and sometimes irrelevant) details to the paragraph, B is the only sentence that properly ties up the ideas in the paragraph.

Most importantly, wear your seat belt at all times. Second, keep your eyes on the road. Do not become distracted by events happening off the road or in your car. Third, make sure that your brakes and tires are in good working order. Fourth, check the gauges on the dashboard frequently for signs of trouble. Finally, make sure your car is clean and orderly so you can have an enjoyable driving experience. [2]

2. Which of the following sentences would best introduce this paragraph?
   F. There are several key points to remember when driving a motor vehicle.
   G. The car is the greatest invention of all times, and it takes skill to operate one.
   H. Driving on a main interstate can be nerve-wracking, but it is a usually quicker route.
   J. Checking that your car always has gas in it will ensure you don't break down somewhere.

The correct answer is F. While the other sentences relate to vehicles, they do not deal with the main idea of the passage, which is what to do when you are driving.

Practice 1: Paragraphs

Directions: Some of the words and phrases in the following passage have been underlined and numbered. The matching questions offer alternatives for the underlined portion. You can choose one of these, or select NO CHANGE if the original wording in the passage is best. If a number appears in a box within the text, the corresponding question will ask about a section of the text that is not underlined (such as a whole paragraph). To choose the best answer for any question, you should read more than just the underlined portion.

A Crisis in Our Schools

[1]

They have sacrificed high corporate salaries, cars that stay together without duct tape, and the perfect nine-to-five job. Teachers have chosen to become parents to one hundred children, not just their own 2.5 children. And they do it for fewer dollars per year than the mechanic who keeps their cars taped together. [1]

Organization, Unity, and Coherence

[2]

The community has been complaining about the lack of quality education in our schools. Parents say teachers need to be held accountable for their children's education. However, many people do not believe the problem is with teachers. No, the problem is much broader than teacher accountability. [2]

[3]

Communities can never repay teachers for such sacrifices, but they can stop complaining and pitch in. We need to quit complaining about our tax money, cut through the red tape, and get more support for our schools and teachers. You and I can do without a new set of golf clubs if it means helping our children and our neighbors' children succeed in life. In fact, we could spend less time on the golf course and more time tutoring children that need extra help in their studies. [3] [4]

1. What sentence best introduces Paragraph 1?

    A. Teachers have to be willing to give up a life of luxury to go into their profession.

    B. Teachers are considered heroes in the eyes of their students and the community.

    C. Students have to give up their social lives if they want to do well in school.

    D. Students should not be held responsible for possessing poor learning habits.

2. What sentence is best added to Paragraph 2?

    F. Teachers should be willing to work long hours to get their lesson plans completed.

    G. Teachers claim that parents also have a responsibility in their child's education.

    H. Teachers demand more money for every year they work in the school system.

    J. Teachers are not responsible for anyone's well-being but their own.

3. What sentence best concludes Paragraph 3?
   A. Community leaders should step up and teach their own children.
   B. The new golf course is now offering discounts for new members.
   C. Students are the pride and joy of our community and should be treated as such.
   D. It takes many concerned, committed people to educate a group of children.

4. What order should these paragraphs go in?
   F. NO CHANGE   G. 1, 3, 2   H. 2, 1, 3   J. 3, 2, 1

DEVELOPING COHERENCE

Not only do paragraphs have to make sense on their own, they must also make sense together as a whole. They must have coherence. **Coherence** means sticking together. The ideas in an essay should "stick together," that is, be connected and lead from one to the other in a logical way. Tying ideas together is an important step an author takes to help readers understand his writing. Authors achieve coherence in many ways, including planning an order and using transitions.

ORGANIZING IDEAS

Organizing ideas in a certain order is the first step to developing coherence. If something is out of order or doesn't belong, it can confuse the reader and interfere with the understanding of what an author wrote. Look at the following example.

> I was walking home. They were pushing and slapping the little guy. I didn't know what I would do when I got there, but I broke into a run toward them. One of the bullies threw the kid's book bag aside. Suddenly I noticed two big guys tormenting a kid that lives down the block from me.

Notice how the events seem out of sequence. How might you change this paragraph? Take a look at the revised example below in which the sentences have been rearranged.

> I was walking home. Suddenly I noticed two big guys tormenting a kid that lives down the block from me. They were pushing and slapping the little guy. One of the bullies threw the kid's book bag aside. I didn't know what I would do when I got there, but I broke into a run toward them.

Organization, Unity, and Coherence

As you can see, **organizational patterns** help writers give direction to their ideas. Using an appropriate pattern can help readers understand the purpose of the piece of writing. Here are the most common patterns.

Organizational Pattern	Description and Example
Chronological order	gives information in time order (as events happened or as a process should be followed) • autobiographical narrative about an event that happened to you
Cause and effect	shows direct relationships, such as an event and its cause(s) and/or effect(s) • research paper about the result of an experiment
Problem and solution	looks at a problem and possible solution(s); similar to cause and effect • persuasive essay that proposes a way to decrease traffic accidents
Comparison and/or contrast	tells about similarities and/or differences between things or ideas • reflective paper that compares a character's journey in a book to an experience in your own life
Order of importance	offers information from most important to least (or vice versa) • expository essay about getting ready for a trip
Classification/division order	divides information into groups or categories • response to literature that explains types of poetry at a specific time in history
Logical order	presents information in the order that makes the most sense for a plot or sequence • mystery story that includes flashbacks and foreshadowing
Spatial order	arranges items by physical positions or relationships • essay describing the carvings on Mount Rushmore

Look at this sample question.

[1] The high winds and rains caused extensive flooding and damage.[2] Hurricane Katrina struck the coastal Louisiana town in the middle of the night.[3] Numerous injuries were reported in addition to many deaths.[4] It swept violently through the town destroying homes and businesses.

1. Which of the following sequences of sentences will make this paragraph flow most logically?

    A. 1, 2, 3, 4   **B.** 4, 3, 2, 1   **C.** 3, 2, 4, 1   **D.** 2, 4, 1, 3

The best answer is D. Sentence 2 is obviously the topic sentence, as it introduces the idea of Hurricane Katrina. The other sentence orders do not make logical sense.

USING TRANSITIONS

Writers use **organizational patterns** so that their writing makes sense to the reader. One tool that writers use to create structure is the transition. **Transitions** may be individual words, or they may be phrases. Transitions show that ideas are connected and how they are connected. Transitions help readers understand what they read. They act as signals for how ideas go together. Familiarize yourself with the following explanations and lists of commonly used transitional words and phrases.

SEQUENCE OF EVENTS

When writers use **sequence of events**, they arrange the details of a story in the order in which they happened. This is also called **time order** or **chronological order**. Sequence of events can go from the first to the last event or from the last to the first event. Usually, stories will be arranged from the first to the last event. Think of the last time a friend told you a personal story. Did she use time order? Did she tell the story from the first to the last event or the other way around? Below are some transition words and phrases that are often used to show a sequence of events.

Sequence of Events Transitions		
after	finally	then
at last	first	thereafter
at once	meanwhile	when
eventually	next	

Organization, Unity, and Coherence

CAUSE-EFFECT

Cause-effect is another organizational structure that writers use. Cause-effect shows how events in a story relate to one another. A **cause** makes something happen. An **effect** is what happens due to the cause. What is the cause-effect relationship between good diet and health? What is the cause-effect relationship between poor study habits and poor grades? What other cause-effect relationships can you think of? The following are transitional words and phrases that are often used to show cause-effect:

Cause and Effect Transitions		
accordingly	due to	so
as a result	for example	so that is why
because	for that reason	therefore
consequently	hence	thus

COMPARE AND CONTRAST

Writers also use **comparison and contrast** to organize ideas. When writers compare and contrast ideas, they show how these ideas are both alike and different. For example, how would you compare and contrast skateboarding and bicycle riding? What about middle school and elementary school? Below are some transitions that are commonly used for comparison and contrast.

Comparing Ideas Transitions			
also	another	like	similarly
and	in addition	likewise	too

Contrasting Ideas Transitions			
but	in spite of	not	unlike
however	instead	on the other hand	while

USING CONJUNCTIVE ADVERBS

Another type of transition is the conjunctive adverb. **Conjunctive adverbs** are used to connect independent clauses. When connecting independent clauses, use a semicolon followed by the conjunctive adverb and then a comma. Conjunctive adverbs show logical relationships, such as cause-effect, sequence, contrast, comparison and so on.

Chapter 3

Common conjunctive adverbs are listed below:

also	anyway	besides	consequently
finally	furthermore	however	incidentally
indeed	instead	likewise	meanwhile
moreover	namely	nevertheless	next
now	otherwise	similarly	still
then	therefore	thus	

Examples: Oliver decided to end his search for the exotic plant; *consequently*, he had more time to devote to his family.

King Sargon knew he ruled a great and powerful nation; *namely*, he did not fear attacks from other countries.

Sometimes conjunctive adverbs are used to link ideas in separate sentences or even separate paragraphs. It is essential to choose the best adverb for your purpose. Look at this example.

Incorrect Example: Melinda was thirty minutes late for her curfew. *Instead*, her parents grounded her for the weekend.

Instead is not the proper conjunctive adverb to use here. It does not make sense, nor does it create the logical relationship between the two sentences. Look at the corrected example.

Correct Example: Melinda was thirty minutes late for her curfew. *Therefore*, her parents grounded her for the weekend.

Do you see how using a different conjunctive adverb makes the relationship between the ideas much clearer?

Look at some sample questions.

[1] Bookmarks are a thoughtful homemade gift that nearly everyone can use. [2] Decorate the bookmark with markers, stickers, pictures cut from magazines, or even photographs. [3] Making a bookmark is a fun and easy project. [4] You can start with any type and color of paper, though stiff paper will work best. [5] To make the bookmark last longer, cover it in clear contact paper.

1. Which of the following sequences of sentences will make the paragraph flow most logically?
   A. NO CHANGE **B.** 2, 3, 1, 5, 4 **C.** 3, 1, 4, 2, 5 **D.** 5, 1, 4, 2, 3

Organization, Unity, and Coherence

The correct answer is C. The logical order for this paragraph is a sequence of events. The other answer choices do not make a clear paragraph.

The trees that line our streets are beautiful, but they are also a danger. Just last week, falling tree limbs knocked over several power lines, endangering the lives of motorists and pedestrians. <u>Nevertheless,</u> I propose that the city start trimming the tree branches on a regular basis.
2

    F. NO CHANGE   **G.** Moreover   **H.** Still   **J.** However

The correct answer is G. Answers F, H, and J make the sentence a contradictory thought from the previous statements.

Practice 2: Coherence

Directions: Some portions in the following passage have been underlined and numbered. The matching questions offer alternatives for the underlined portion. You can choose one of these, or select NO CHANGE if the original version in the passage is best. If a number appears in a box within the text, the corresponding question will ask about a section of the text that is not underlined (such as a whole paragraph). To choose the best answer for any question, you should read more than just the underlined portion.

[1] Communication between the lower forty-eight states and the frigid Arctic region was especially difficult. [2] During the Klondike gold rush, Alaska was a wild, untamed territory. [3] This method of mail delivery made life easier for the miners of the Klondike gold rush. [4] Mail carriers rode in dogsleds and raced along the white expanse delivering mail and medicine. [5] <u>Conversely,</u> dogsleds were able to improve communication greatly. ☐2☐

1.
    A. NO CHANGE   **B.** Instead   **C.** Otherwise   **D.** However

2. Which of the following sequences of sentences will make this paragraph flow most logically?
    F. NO CHANGE
    G. 2, 1, 5, 4, 3
    H. 5, 4, 3, 2, 1
    J. 4, 2, 1, 3, 5

Chapter 3

[1] Hand grippers can help give your arms the bulging muscles you're after, but only if they offer enough resistance. [2] If you can squeeze them repeatedly for one to two minutes and your hands don't get tired, they're too weak for you. [3] You can keep buying stronger ones or make something at home that can do the same job. [4] Consequently, there are many household items you can use to make effective hand grippers. 4 5

3. **A.** NO CHANGE
    B. Meanwhile
    C. Thus
    D. Incidentally

4. Which of the following sequences of sentences will make this paragraph flow most logically?
    F. NO CHANGE
    G. 4, 3, 2, 1
    H. 2, 1, 4, 3
    J. 3, 2, 1, 4

Question 5 asks about the preceding paragraph as a whole.

5. Which sentence could be logically added to the beginning of this paragraph?
    A. Have you ever wanted buff biceps like the famous body builders?
    B. Hand grippers are instruments you can hold in your hands.
    C. Did you know that your arm has over twenty muscles?
    D. Protein will help build and tone your muscles.

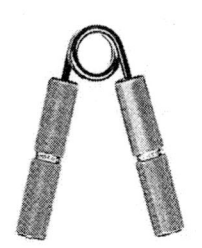

Organization, Unity, and Coherence

> ## CHAPTER 3 SUMMARY
>
> A **paragraph** is a group of sentences that are related.
>
> The ideas of an essay should "stick together," that is, have **coherence**.
>
> **Organizational patterns** help writers give direction to their ideas.
>
> **Transitions** are words or phrases that show ideas that are connected and how they are connected.
>
> When writers use **sequence of events**, they arrange the details of a story in the order in which they happened. This is also called **time order** or **chronological order**.
>
> **Cause-effect** shows how events in a story relate to one another. A **cause** makes something happen. An **effect** is what happens due to the cause.
>
> When writers **compare and contrast** ideas, they show how these ideas are both alike and different.
>
> **Conjunctive adverbs** show logical relationships, such as cause-effect, sequence of events, contrast and comparison, and so on.

CHAPTER 3 REVIEW

Directions: Some portions in the following passage have been underlined and numbered. The matching questions in the right-hand column offer alternatives for the underlined portion. You can choose one of these, or select NO CHANGE if the original version in the passage is best. If a number appears in a box within the text, the corresponding question will ask about a section of the text that is not underlined (such as a whole paragraph). To choose the best answer for any question, you should read more than just the underlined portion.

The Presidential Election Process

[1]

Before having the opportunity to win a general election to become the president of the United States, each of the major party's candidates must <u>lastly</u> be nominated by their
₁
party's nomination convention. The convention meets about three months before the election. Delegates from all the states assemble to nominate candidates for the offices of president and vice president. [2]

[2]

[1] On Election Day, voters go to the polls. [2] The voters then vote for electors, whom in turn vote for candidates. [3] In most states, the ballot lists the names of the nominees rather than the names of the electors. [4] Once nominated, the presidential candidates then begin the eight-to-ten-week campaign for the general election. [5] Election Day is held on the first Tuesday in November (or the Tuesday after the first Monday in leap years). [6] Therefore, many people believe they are actually voting for the presidential candidates. [3]

1. A. NO CHANGE
   B. first
   C. secondly
   D. next

2. Which sentence best introduces Paragraph 1?
   F. The presidential election has had many processes before concluding with the one we know.
   G. There is much to understand about the presidential candidates before you cast your vote.
   H. The presidential candidates to be voted on are nominated by each political party.
   J. The presidential election as we know it is actually more complicated than perceived.

3. Which of the following sequences of sentences will make Paragraph 2 flow most logically?
   A. NO CHANGE
   B. 5, 2, 3, 1, 6, 4
   C. 4, 5, 1, 2, 3, 6
   D. 6, 1, 4, 2, 3, 5

Organization, Unity, and Coherence

[3]

As explained before, the president and vice president are actually elected by electors from each state that comprises the Electoral College. <u>Contrary to popular belief</u>, an elector is not obligated to vote for the candidate he or she originally indicated. The 538 electors are free to vote for whomever they wish when they gather to officially vote. However, it is extremely rare for an elector to not vote for whom he or she originally indicated. [5] [6]

4. F. NO CHANGE
   G. According to popular belief
   H. In addition
   J. Therefore

5. Which sentence best concludes Paragraph 3?
   A. Inauguration Day is held on January 20 of the following year.
   B. The Electoral College was established to prevent a president from winning by popular vote.
   C. A candidate must receive at least 270 votes to be elected to the office of president or vice president.
   D. Presidential candidates must choose their vice-presidential running mate early in the campaign.

   > Question 6 asks about the preceding passage as a whole.

6. Suppose the writer wanted to add the following sentence to the essay:
   > Each state has a number of electors equal to the number of their senators and representatives.

   This sentence would most logically fit into:
   F. Paragraph 2.
   G. Paragraph 3.
   H. the beginning of Paragraph 1.
   J. the end of Paragraph 1.

Chapter 3

Organization, Unity, and Coherence

Chapter 4
Word Choice

Word choice questions on the PLAN English Test earn points in the following way, ranging from fundamental skills in word choice (up to 15 score points) to sophisticated skills in word choice (28–32 points):

Points	Benchmark Description
13–15	Revise sentences to correct awkward and confusing arrangements of sentence elements Revise vague nouns and pronouns that create obvious logic problems
16–19	Delete obviously synonymous and wordy material in a sentence Revise expressions that deviate from the style of an essay
20–23	Delete redundant material when information is repeated in different parts of speech (e.g., "alarmingly startled") Use the word or phrase most consistent with the style and tone of a fairly straightforward essay Determine the clearest and most logical conjunction to link clauses
24–27	Revise a phrase that is redundant in terms of the meaning and logic of the entire sentence Identify and correct ambiguous pronoun references Use the word or phrase most appropriate in terms of the content of the sentence and tone of the essay
28–32	Correct redundant material that involves sophisticated vocabulary and sounds acceptable as conversational English (e.g., "an aesthetic viewpoint" versus "the outlook of an aesthetic viewpoint") Correct vague and wordy or clumsy and confusing writing containing sophisticated language

As you have probably learned throughout your time in school, the words you choose when you write are vital to comprehension. Not only does the correct **word choice** give your writing style and flair, but it also ensures your writing is clear and consistent.

Word Choice

On the PLAN English Test, you will be presented with a passage that is in need of revision. It may have redundant material that needs to be deleted, or it could contain expressions that stray from the style of the essay. In any case, you will need to be able to recognize these errors and correct them. This chapter will review how to best choose your words based on **style**, **tone**, **clarity**, and **economy**.

WRITING WITH STYLE

What do you think about when you see the word *style*? Writing is probably not the first thing that comes to mind. If you're thinking of style as it relates to fashion, then it would mean keeping up with the latest trends. If you're thinking of style as a way of expressing yourself, then it would mean standing out from the rest of the crowd. But what does it mean to write with style?

Style is the control of language that is appropriate to the purpose, audience, and context of the writing task. A writer's style is evident through both word choice and sentence fluency. Look at the two examples below. Can you tell by analyzing the choice of words and the flow of the sentences which paragraph was written for a children's story and which was written for an encyclopedia?

Example 1:

Buckwheat is grown in Great Britain only to supply food for pheasants and to feed poultry, which devour the seeds with avidity. In the northern countries of Europe, however, the seeds are employed as human food, chiefly in the form of cakes, which when baked thin have an agreeable taste, with a darkish, somewhat violet color. The meal of buckwheat is also baked into crumpets, as a favorite dainty among Dutch children, and in the Russian army buckwheat groats are served out as part of the soldiers' rations, which they cook with butter, tallow, or hemp-seed oil.

Example 2:

In the summer, the thick undergrowth, the intertwining vines, and the heavy lower branches of the trees, make it difficult even to see into the dark recesses of the forest. But in the winter all is open. The low wet places, the deep holes, the rotten bogs, everything on the ground that is in the way of a good run and a jump, is covered up. You do not walk a hundred yards under the bare branches of the trees before up starts a rabbit, or a hare, if you would rather call him by his right name,—and away go the dogs, and away you go—all of you tearing along at the top of your speed!

Let's look at some phrases used in the first paragraph: *devour the seeds with avidity, an agreeable taste*, and *buckwheat groats are served out*. These words and phrases are descriptive, but they are less personal and more formal and informative in nature. They describe ideas and actions but not in a way that evokes emotion or imagination. The purpose of the paragraph is to inform. The audience is anyone who is interested in knowing the cultural uses of buckwheat. In what kind of publication do you think you would find this paragraph? If you said *encyclopedia*, you're right! You could find this article in an encyclopedia under the entry *Buckwheat*.

Now let's look at some of the phrases used in the second paragraph: *intertwining vines, a good run and a jump, away go the dogs, and away you go*, and *tearing along*. You can tell here that the writer wants the reader emotionally involved and, in this case, excited! The writer uses words and phrases in a more informal sense, and the reader is encouraged to envision what is taking place. This paragraph is quite different than the first paragraph. Its purpose is to entertain. Its audience is anyone who would like to chase a rabbit through the woods—probably a child (or someone who is childlike). In what kind of publication do you think you would find this paragraph? If you said a fiction book, then you're right! This paragraph is taken from a children's storybook by Frank Richard Stockton called *Round-about Rambles in Lands of Fact and Fancy*.

These two paragraphs are both very well written; the vocabulary used is both precise and purposeful. And even though they were written for two very different reasons, they were both written with style. As we have just seen, each paragraph demonstrates its writer's control of the language that was most appropriate for the purpose, audience, and context.

This next example of writing demonstrates a lack of attention to its purpose, audience, and context. The writing prompt for this example is to write a paragraph for your school newspaper defining the concept of family, using examples from your own experience.

Example:

A family is a group of people that relate to you. The people in your family may or may not be real close to you, but they are almost always there for you. Not long ago, I went through some very rough times, and my family had my back even when my friends didn't. If I ever go through anything bad again, I know I can count on my family. Family also reminds you of who you are. Everybody needs to have a family.

Word Choice

Notice how the use of nonspecific phrases (*relate to you, real close, rough times, count on my family*) makes the purpose of the paragraph seem unfocused. There is little indication that the writer has the audience in mind (friendship is devalued though it is probably very important to the audience). Examples from the author's experience are lacking, and there is little in the paragraph that demonstrates a precise and purposeful vocabulary.

Writing with style involves knowing what doesn't belong in a body of text as much as knowing what does belong. With a careful eye, you can spot expressions, words, and phrases that don't fit in with the style of a body of text. Consider the following passage:

[1] Mockingbirds are common and popular birds in the eastern and southern regions of the United States. [2] The mockingbird is the state bird of Arkansas, Florida, Mississippi, Tennessee, and Texas. [3] My grandpa calls them "mockers," because it's so funny how they copy other animal noises. [4] They are known for their ability to mimic other birds, mammals, and insects with song and sounds. [5] Mockingbirds often live close to human homes, nesting in ornamental hedges.

Which sentence deviates from the overall style of the passage?

A. Sentence 1
B. Sentence 2
C. Sentence 3
D. Sentence 5

The correct answer is C. The passage has a straightforward, formal style. Its purpose is to inform the reader about mockingbirds. Answer C uses the first person (*My grandpa*) and informal, personal language (*it's so funny*) that feels out of place in a formal essay.

CHOOSING THE RIGHT WORDS

Let's continue to consider style, now as it relates to **word choice**. One aspect of good word choice is selecting specific and concrete words rather than general or abstract words. When you use clear, precise words, you create vivid writing.

Avoid vague, overused words such as *thing, nice, great, bad, good, awesome,* and *a lot*. These words have many meanings, but none is very clear or specific. Specific words provide the reader with a clear image of what you describe.

Chapter 4

When you are writing a description, using adjectives, adverbs, or verbs that involve the senses will convey your exact meaning. Think of what you want the reader to see, hear, feel, smell, and taste. For example, you might write the following sentence:

> The Beowulf College fans showed excitement at the football game.

To make this sentence more descriptive, you could write the sentence this way:

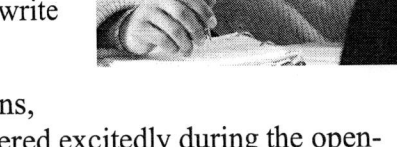

> The passionate Beowulf College fans, dressed head to toe in red and gold, cheered excitedly during the opening kickoff of the homecoming football game.

In the new sentence, the word *passionate* and the phrase *dressed head to toe in red and gold* describe the fans and create a strong visual image. The vivid verb/adverb combination *cheered excitedly* replaces the dull phrase *showed excitement* and clarifies the action of the fans. Adding the prepositional phrases *at the opening kickoff* and *of the homecoming game* describes the time frame and the significance of the game.

Read this excerpt from *The War of the Worlds*. Pay close attention to how H. G. Wells paints a vivid picture for his readers with the words he chooses.

Example:

> A moderate incline runs towards the foot of Maybury Hill, and down this we clattered. Once the lightning had begun, it went on in as rapid a succession of flashes as I have ever seen. The thunderclaps, treading one on the heels of another and with a strange crackling accompaniment, sounded more like the working of a gigantic electric machine than the usual detonating reverberations. The flickering light was blinding and confusing, and a thin hail smote gustily at [the windshield] as I drove down the slope.
>
> –H. G. Wells, *The War of the Worlds*

Now look at these sample questions.

1. Marcus wanted a new video game, but he didn't have any money.

   A. NO CHANGE
   B. Marcus liked playing video games, and he was tired of all the old ones he already had.
   C. Marcus longed to try his hand at the new adventure game, but his wallet was empty.
   D. What Marcus really wanted was a new game and a new system on which to play it.

Word Choice

The best answer is C. The sentence uses descriptive language (*try his hand, adventure game, his wallet was empty*) that makes the writing more interesting to read. Answers B and D change the meaning of the original sentence; they indicate that Marcus likes video games, but they don't explain that he can't afford to buy a new one.

2. Sally made a lot of money last year selling seashells.
   F. NO CHANGE
   G. Selling seashells by the seashore, Sally made some money and saw dolphins swimming.
   H. To earn money for college, Sally sold nice seashells, but she hated the bad smell of fish.
   J. Last summer, Sally earned nearly three hundred dollars selling brightly patterned starfish, cockles, and conch shells to Laguna Beach tourists.

The correct answer is J. The other choices use vague words (like *some*, *nice*, and *bad*) and add irrelevant details.

Practice 1: Style

Directions: Some portions in the following passage have been underlined and numbered. The matching questions offer alternatives for the underlined portion. You can choose one of these, or select NO CHANGE if the original version in the passage is best. If a number appears in a box within the text, the corresponding question will ask about a section of the text that is not underlined (such as a whole paragraph). To choose the best answer for any question, you should read more than just the underlined portion.

The Goliath Bird-Eating Spider

The Goliath bird-eating spider is one of the largest spiders in the world. These spiders, which are in the tarantula group of arachnids, can measure <u>very long</u>. Goliath birdeaters are native to
1
the rainforests of South America, and they usually live near swamps or marshes. These large spiders got their name from explorers who saw a Goliath birdeater <u>gobble up</u> a hummingbird.
2
Some of these spiders may also eat rats, lizards, and other spiders. Although it is <u>the Hercules
3
of the arachnid world</u>, this spider is not dangerous to humans. A Goliath generally will not attack humans unless it is <u>ticked off</u>, and <u>if you get bitten by one, it's no worse than if you get
4   5
stung by a wasp</u>.

1. A. NO CHANGE
   B. a good length
   C. up to eleven inches long
   D. a nice amount of inches

2. F. NO CHANGE
   G. consume
   H. snack on
   J. scarf down

3. A. NO CHANGE
   B. a big and strong spider
   C. really big
   D. as strong as an elephant

4. F. NO CHANGE
   G. hopping mad
   H. scared silly
   J. provoked

5. A. NO CHANGE
   B. its fangs, dripping poison, scare people, but they only sting like a wasp
   C. its venom is only as dangerous as that of a wasp
   D. its venom isn't so bad

TONE AND MOOD

On the PLAN English Test, you might be asked questions regarding a passage's tone or how a word choice affects the mood of the passage. You must be able to pick out the correct response based on what you know about tone and mood.

In writing, **tone** is the writer's attitude or feeling toward the topic. This attitude can be stated clearly, or it can be implied. A writer can use the same type of language to convey very different tones. The mood of a piece of writing is closely related to writer's tone. The **mood** is the overall atmosphere or feeling of a piece of writing. Both tone and mood are revealed through the writer's choice of words and phrases.

Word Choice

The mood of a piece of writing corresponds with the tone of the writer. If the tone (attitude) of the writer is humorous, then the mood (atmosphere) created by the writing will probably be joyful and lighthearted. If the tone (attitude) of the writer is cynical or sarcastic, then the mood (atmosphere) created by the writing could be funny or irritating, depending on what the reader thinks about the writer's particular point of view. In the previous excerpt from H. G. Wells's *The War of the Worlds*, you could say that the author's tone is fearful and awestruck, creating a suspenseful, uneasy mood for the reader.

To remain clear when trying to differentiate between tone and mood, think of tone and mood in this way: Tone is the attitude expressed by the writer; mood is the atmosphere experienced by the reader.

When reading passages on the PLAN English Test, keep the author's tone and mood in mind. Make your choices based on what best fits that tone and mood. Look at this example.

The Dark Side of College Recruiting

Every year, stories of college athletic programs that are put on probation for violating NCAA recruiting regulations fill the headlines of sports pages across the nation. Scandals abound. Talented athletes are approached and offered illegal gifts of money, cars, material possessions, and so on. Most schools admit that they have athletes who either have accepted illegal gifts or have been approached and offered such gifts. <u>Raking in tons of dough every year</u>, college athletes are more than just students; they are assets to a university. Some critics of the current system might even call them commodities. The coaches who recruit these athletes denounce recruiting violations publicly, but often participate or allow them behind closed doors <u>because they just want the best for the school</u>.

1. **A.** NO CHANGE
    B. Generating millions of dollars in revenue annually
    C. Greedily collecting lots of money each year
    D. Bringing home the bacon year after year

Answer B is correct. Answer C casts the college athletes in a bad light, which doesn't match the author's attitude in the passage. Answer D is colloquial and does not fit in with the formal style of the essay.

2. F. NO CHANGE
   G. because they hold athletic excellence in high regard
   H. and violate the code of ethics
   J. because no one really gets hurt

The correct answer is H because it fits with the speaker's judgmental tone toward these recruiting violations. The other answers make excuses for the illegal activities.

CLARITY

Writers always strive to convey their ideas accurately and in an interesting way to the reader. When a piece of writing has **clarity**, it is cohesive, concise, and easy for the reader to understand. You have already learned how important word choice is for getting your ideas across to the reader. Another way to enhance clarity involves revising sentences to improve logic and flow. Awkward arrangements of sentence elements, ambiguous pronoun references, and illogical conjunctions linking clauses can make a piece of writing confusing to read.

REVISING AWKWARD SENTENCES

Sentences can sound awkward or confusing even if they are not technically incorrect. Whenever possible, read your writing aloud, and pay attention to how smoothly the sentences flow. You will find that sometimes your ears can pick out clumsy, rough text more easily than your eyes. Revising problem text can be a simple matter of tweaking the way the sentence elements are arranged.

Example: Going to the park every day is my goal, which is a good way to get in shape.

In this sentence, it is not clear what the adjective clause "which is a good way to get in shape" is modifying. It looks like it's modifying "my goal," which comes right before the adjective clause.

Correction: It's my goal to go to the park every day, which is a good way to get in shape.

By rewriting the sentence this way, it's now clear that the clause *which is a good way to get in shape* modifies *to go to the park every day.* You will learn more about misplaced modifiers in chapter 5.

See if you can revise the following awkward sentence.

1. Lamar meets Dr. Francis at the office, returning for the first time after a trip to Guam.

   A. NO CHANGE

   B. Returning to the office for the first time after a trip to Guam, Lamar meets Dr. Francis.

   C. Lamar meets Dr. Francis at the office. He is returning for the first time after a trip to Guam.

   D. Returning for the first time after a trip to Guam, at the office, where Lamar meets Dr. Francis.

Answer B is correct. Answer C does not make it clear who is returning from Guam, and D does not contain an independent clause.

AVOIDING VAGUE PRONOUNS

Pronouns (*I, you, he, she, it, we,* and *they,* among others) take the place of a noun. A writer can cause confusion when pronouns are misplaced, making them seemingly refer to the wrong person. You never want to force a reader to guess to whom or what a pronoun is referring.

Example: He was looking to sign a message to Koko, the gorilla, but in studying her movements, she did not behave as though interested in eating at the moment.

As the sentence stands, the gorilla is studying her own behavior as the modifying prepositional phrase *in studying her movements* comes immediately before the pronoun *she*. Logically, this sentence does not make sense.

Correct: He was looking to sign a message to Koko, the gorilla, but a study of her behavior showed she behaved as though not interested in eating at the moment.

By rewording the sentence, it becomes clear that the *he* of the sentence is the man observing Koko's behavior.

Look at the next example.

2. Jasmine played a trick on Becky. <u>She told her that John wanted to date her</u> when he really didn't.

   F. NO CHANGE

   G. Jasmine told her that John wanted to date her

   H. She told Becky that John wanted to date Becky

   J. Becky told her that John wanted to date Jasmine

Answer H is correct. It makes it clear that Jasmine told Becky that John wanted to date Becky. The other answers leave it unclear as to whom the pronouns "she" and "her" refer. Answer J doesn't work because it has Becky playing the trick on Jasmine instead of the other way around. However, since repeating the name Becky twice is redundant, the sentences might be better rewritten.

USING LOGICAL CONJUNCTIONS

As you will review further in chapter 5, **conjunctions** such as *for*, *and*, *nor*, *but*, *or*, *yet*, and *so* are words which join two or more independent clauses in a sentence. You can use a conjunction in place of a semicolon to join two clauses together. The trick is to choose the clearest and most logical conjunction for that sentence. Consider the following example:

1. Dennis watched the fireworks display from <u>seventy feet away, but he would be safe</u>.

   A. NO CHANGE

   B. seventy feet away, or he would be safe

   C. seventy feet away, yet he would be safe

   D. seventy feet away, so he would be safe

Answer D is correct: Dennis watched the fireworks display from seventy feet away, *so* he would be safe. The first clause allows the second clause to happen. The other answers contradict the logical message of the sentence.

Word Choice

Practice 2: Clarity

Directions: Some portions in the following passage have been underlined and numbered. The matching questions offer alternatives for the underlined portion. You can choose one of these, or select NO CHANGE if the original version in the passage is best. If a number appears in a box within the text, the corresponding question will ask about a section of the text that is not underlined (such as a whole paragraph). To choose the best answer for any question, you should read more than just the underlined portion.

Flounder Gigging

[1]

When most people think of fishing, they picture a father and son standing on the shore, or perhaps sitting in a boat, with fishing poles in hand and lines cast. Seeking to haul in an enormous swordfish or tuna, some might also picture a large fishing boat with professional fishermen.
1
But in the coastal sounds along the shores of states like North Carolina, it often takes
2
on a different look. Instead of grabbing a fishing pole or a large net, some arm themselves with a long, spear-like pole, known as a gig. These fishermen engage in a common form of fishing known as "flounder gigging."

[2]

Flounder are flat fish that lay on the ocean floor in the shallow sounds along the Atlantic coast. Late at night, usually during low tide, "giggers" will stand on the bow of a small boat. No motor is used, but the flounder aren't scared away. As the gigger stands at the front of the
3
boat (with a lantern or flashlight casting light over the water so that he or she can see the sound floor), another person stands at the rear of the boat, pushing it along as quietly as possible with a paddle or long pole. When the gigger sees a flounder, they quickly jabs it with the gig and
4
pulls it into the boat.

Chapter 4

1. **A.** NO CHANGE
   B. Some might also picture a large fishing boat, seeking to haul in an enormous swordfish or tuna, with professional fishermen.
   C. Some might also picture a large fishing boat with professional fishermen seeking to haul in an enormous swordfish or tuna.
   D. Some, seeking to haul in an enormous swordfish or tuna, might also picture a large fishing boat with professional fishermen.

2. **F.** NO CHANGE **G.** fishermen **H.** swordfish **J.** fishing

3. **A.** NO CHANGE **B.** yet **C.** so **D.** for

4. **F.** NO CHANGE **G.** he **H.** it **J.** the flounder

ECONOMY

To write in a clear, straightforward manner, writers exercise **economy** by looking for ways to be concise. There's no sense in using five words in a phrase when two words will get the point across more directly. As you read and write, consider how succinct or how wordy a piece of text appears to be. While it's important as a writer to use precise, descriptive language to paint a vivid picture of what you're describing, you also need to avoid **wordiness** to ensure your writing is clear and concise. Some phrases simply pad your writing without adding anything of significant value. To eliminate wordiness, remember that positive sentences are clearer for readers than negative ones, and dropping common empty phrases like *the fact that* fosters concise writing.

In the following examples, wordy phrases and the more concise versions are underlined.

> **Example:** At this moment in time, smartphones are incredibly popular.
>
> **Correction:** Smartphones today are incredibly popular.
>
> **Example:** To make a long story short, the perceived global hoarding of oil, which is at a crisis level, is pricing energy beyond the reach of many third world nations.
>
> **Correction:** The perceived global hoarding of oil, now at crisis levels, is pricing energy beyond the reach of many third world nations.

Word Choice

Look at this sample question:

1. Although Marjorie went shopping last weekend <u>for the purpose of expanding</u> her wardrobe, she couldn't find an outfit she liked this morning.

    A. NO CHANGE

    B. desirous of expanding

    C. so that she might expand

    D. to expand

The correct answer is D. The phrase *to expand* is the simplest, most concise way of explaining why Marjorie went to the store. Answer C is just as wordy as the phrase in the original sentence. Answer B slightly alters the meaning of the sentence; *desirous of* is a verbose way of saying *wanting to*.

You also need to cut out obviously **synonymous** or **redundant** material in a sentence. When you're repeating the same information in different parts of speech ("We were unexpectedly surprised"), the effect is unnecessary wordiness. Sometimes the redundant material is difficult to spot because it involves sophisticated language and sounds acceptable as conversational English.

Example: She set out to write an autobiography of her own life.

The phrase *autobiography of her own life* is redundant because an autobiography is an account of someone's life written by that person. Adding *of her own life* is unnecessary because she wouldn't be writing an autobiography of anyone else's life.

Correction: She set out to write an autobiography.

This corrected sentence reads more clearly because it does not restate the same idea.

Look at the following sentence.

2. Louis put his life in jeopardy by driving recklessly, which could have killed him.
    F. NO CHANGE

    G. Driving recklessly could have killed Louis, who put his life in jeopardy.

    H. Louis drove recklessly, putting his life in jeopardy because it could kill him.

    J. Louis put his life in jeopardy by driving recklessly.

The correct answer is J. The clause *which could have killed him* is redundant because it restates the fact that Louis put his life in jeopardy; it can be dropped to make the sentence more concise.

Chapter 4

Practice 3: Economy

Directions: Some portions in the following passage have been underlined and numbered. The matching questions offer alternatives for the underlined portion. You can choose one of these, or select NO CHANGE if the original version in the passage is best. If a number appears in a box within the text, the corresponding question will ask about a section of the text that is not underlined (such as a whole paragraph). To choose the best answer for any question, you should read more than just the underlined portion.

Why You Need a Compost Pile in Your Backyard

[1]

The home compost pile is an <u>efficiently productive</u> mulch factory, and mulch is very valuable
                                                   1
in a garden. <u>With the use of</u> mulch, your garden will look more attractive and have fewer weeds.
             2
The mulch keeps moisture in the soil and also acts as an insulator. It keeps the soil temperature

more consistent. Mulch can also be used <u>in order to</u> disguise bare dirt in the garden.
                                          3

[2]

The process of decomposing plant matter into mulch takes time. That is why gardeners

usually have several compost piles "cooking" at various stages of <u>rotting decomposition</u>. <u>In lieu</u>
                                                                       4   5
<u>of</u> putting grass clippings and leaves in the landfill, they can be composted and recycled back

into your garden as mulch. Chemical fertilizers put on the lawn and absorbed by the grass then

get recycled through the compost pile. As <u>an added bonus,</u> a compost pile benefits from some
                                              6
types of kitchen waste. These include potato and carrot peelings, coffee grounds, and egg

shells. Putting those items in a compost pile is more ecologically friendly than sending them to

the local landfill.

1.   A. NO CHANGE   C. efficient
         B. efficient and productive   D. productively efficient

2.   F. NO CHANGE   H. With regards to using
         G. By using   J. As a consequence of using

Word Choice

3. A. NO CHANGE
    B. for the purpose of
    C. to
    D. as a means of

4. F. NO CHANGE
    G. decomposition
    H. rotten decomposition
    J. decomposing rot

5. A. NO CHANGE
    B. In place of
    C. As opposed to
    D. Rather than

6. F. NO CHANGE
    G. an extra addition
    H. a bonus
    J. another plus

CHAPTER 4 SUMMARY

Style is the control of language that is appropriate to the purpose, audience, and context of the writing task. A writer's style is evident through both word choice and sentence fluency.

To improve your **word choice**, try to answer the questions *Who?*, *What?*, *Where?*, *When?*, *Why?*, and *How?* in as much detail as you can.

Avoid **vague**, overused words such as *thing, nice, great, bad, good, awesome,* and *a lot*; choose specific, **concrete words** that provide a clear image of what you're describing.

Tone is the attitude expressed by the writer; **mood** is the atmosphere experienced by the reader.

Choose words and phrases that are appropriate to the overall tone and style of the text.

When a piece of writing has **clarity**, it is cohesive, concise, and easy for the reader to understand. Clarity can be improved by revising sentences to correct awkward arrangements of sentence elements such as misplaced modifiers, ambiguous pronoun references, and illogical conjunctions.

To write in a clear, straightforward manner, exercise **economy** and look for ways to be **concise**. Avoid **wordiness** and **redundant material** in your writing.

CHAPTER 4 REVIEW

Directions: Some portions in the following passage have been underlined and numbered. The matching questions in the right-hand column offer alternatives for the underlined portion. You can choose one of these, or select NO CHANGE if the original version in the passage is best. If a number appears in a box within the text, the corresponding question will ask about a section of the text that is not underlined (such as a whole paragraph). To choose the best answer for any question, you should read more than just the underlined portion.

Lacrosse

[1]

Baseball may be America's iconic pastime, but lacrosse is one of the few modern sports that originated in North America. The North American Indians in what is today the United States and Canada developed the sport around the twelfth century, though its roots may go back further than that. Lacrosse legend states that the game was played to end disputes and to prepare young men for war. European settlers became <u>attentively interested</u> in the sport after watching the Native Americans play. It wasn't until the late

1.   A. NO CHANGE
    B. interested and attentive
    C. interested
    D. interestingly attentive

Word Choice

1800s that Canadian dentist W. George Beers created <u>the rules and regulations. These rules and regulations became the basis for the modern sport</u>.
                              2

[2]

Today, many people around the world enjoy playing and watching this <u>really neat</u> game.
                                                       3
The two-team sport uses a small rubber ball. Each player has a long-handled stick (called a cross or lacrosse stick) <u>with an oblong, netted pocket to catch the ball on one end of it</u>. As in hockey or football (soccer),
                4

the objective is to get <u>it</u> into the goal of the
                         5
opposing team. Lacrosse is a very physically demanding sport. But today's lacrosse games probably would seem tame by comparison with how they started.

2. **F.** NO CHANGE
   G. the rules and regulations that became the basis for the modern sport
   H. the rules and regulations. These became the basis for the modern sport
   J. the rules and regulations, and these rules then became the basis for the modern sport

3. **A.** NO CHANGE
   B. sweet
   C. thrilling
   D. cool

4. **F.** NO CHANGE
   G. with an oblong, to catch the ball, netted pocket on one end of it
   H. to catch the ball on one end of it with an oblong, netted pocket
   J. with an oblong, netted pocket on one end of it to catch the ball

5. **A.** NO CHANGE
   B. the ball
   C. the stick
   D. the pocket

Chapter 4

[3]

Stories have been told, <u>for</u> a few written
                         6
down, about how tribes in North America
undertook the sport. Those who played were
taking part as warriors on behalf of their
tribes, and <u>they</u> as a whole were dedicated to
            7
"the creator." Early lacrosse balls were larger
than today's standard ball <u>in addition to often
                                8
being made</u> of clay, stone, or wood covered in
deerskin. Teams consisted of up to a hundred
men, with some games having as many as a
thousand <u>bloodthirsty</u> participants. <u>A game
          9   10
could last for days, taking a long time</u>. There
was deep spiritual commitment, as there
would be for battle, and victors brought glory
and honor to their tribes.

6. F. NO CHANGE
   G. yet
   H. and
   J. or

7. A. NO CHANGE
   B. the warriors
   C. the tribes
   D. the games

8. F. NO CHANGE
   G. and often made
   H. in conjunction with often being made
   J. as well as often being made

9. A. NO CHANGE
   B. violent
   C. eager
   D. passive

10. F. NO CHANGE
    G. A game, which took a long time, could last for days
    H. A game could last a long time, taking days
    J. A game could last for days

Word Choice

Chapter 5
Sentence Structure

Sentences structure questions on the PLAN English Test earn points in the following way, ranging from fundamental skills in sentence structure (up to 15 score points) to sophisticated skills in sentence structure (28–32 points):

Points	Benchmark Description
13–15	Use conjunctions or punctuation to join simple clauses
	Revise shifts in verb tense between simple clauses in a sentence or between simple adjoining sentences
16–19	Determine the need for punctuation and conjunctions to avoid awkward-sounding sentence fragments and fused sentences
	Decide the appropriate verb tense and voice by considering the meaning of the entire sentence
20–23	Recognize and correct marked disturbances of sentence flow and structure (e.g., participial phrase fragments, missing or incorrect relative pronouns, dangling or misplaced modifiers)
24–27	Revise to avoid faulty placement of phrases and faulty coordination and subordination of clauses in sentences with subtle structural problems
	Maintain consistent verb tense and pronoun person on the basis of the preceding clause or sentence
28–32	Use sentence-combining techniques, effectively avoiding problematic comma splices, run-on sentences, and sentence fragments, especially in sentences containing compound subjects or verbs
	Maintain a consistent and logical use of verb tense and pronoun person on the basis of information in the paragraph or essay as a whole

SENTENCES

As you have learned in school, a **clause** contains at least one subject and one verb. All sentences are made up of clauses, but some sentences vary in their usage of clauses. An **independent clause** is a group of words with a subject and predicate that can stand on its own as a sentence. A **dependent clause** also has a subject and predicate but cannot stand alone. Remember, there are four main sentence types that use clauses.

A **simple sentence** is formed with one independent clause.

> **Examples:** She enjoys ice skating and skiing.
>
> Jeffrey prefers action films over dramatic ones.

Sentence Structure

When two or more independent clauses are joined, this is a **compound sentence**.

Examples: Mom went to the spa today; she got a facial and a manicure.

Isla is a sophomore, and Ricky is a senior.

Since dependent clauses cannot stand alone, they must be properly connected to independent clauses. A **complex sentence** is a simple sentence with a dependent clause. If the dependent clause comes before the independent clause, it must be set off with a comma. If the independent clause comes first, the sentence does not need a comma.

Examples: When her students finally quieted down, Mrs. Johnston began the history lesson.

Peter wants to be an FBI agent when he grows up.

A compound sentence with a dependent clause is a **compound-complex sentence**.

Examples: Even when she does not feel like it, Carrie always jogs in the morning, and she feels better after doing it.

Before we buy shoes, my mom looks for bargains, but sometimes we splurge.

SENTENCE ERRORS

If a sentence has two independent clauses, the clauses must be joined with the proper punctuation. With no punctuation, the two clauses become a **run-on sentence**, or a **fused sentence**.

Incorrect Example: Yolanda tried to wash her clothes she forgot to put in detergent.

To correct this run-on, there are multiple options. The two clauses can be joined by either a semicolon or a comma and a coordinating conjunction (*and, but, for, nor, so, yet, or*). Or depending on the meaning of the two clauses, splitting them into separate sentences is also an option. Even still, you could make a complex sentence by making one part into a dependent clause

Correct Examples: Yolanda tried to wash her clothes**;** she forgot to put in detergent.

Yolanda tried to wash her clothes**, but** she forgot to put in detergent.

Yolanda tried to wash her clothes**.** She forgot to put in detergent.

When Yolanda tried to wash her clothes**,** she forgot to put in detergent.

Remember, if you are going to use a comma and a conjunction, pick the best conjunction for the meaning of the sentence. In the example above, the conjunction *so* would not have fit. This is an example of **faulty coordination**. The sentences together would have been awkward, and the reader could have misinterpreted the meaning of the sentence.

Chapter 5

Subordination means one idea is subordinate to the other. This means the most important part of the sentence should also be the main part.

Example: I gazed out my window while seeing a car hit a mailbox and then drive away.

The important part of that sentence was that a car hit a mailbox and then drove away. A better way to write this would be like the following:

Correct Example: While gazing out my window, I saw a car hit a mailbox and then drive away.

Comma splices are punctuation errors in which two independent clauses are joined only by a comma, with no conjunction.

Example: You're going to a concert, you can't wear that.

As with run-on sentences, there are several ways to correct comma splices. You can replace the comma with a semicolon, insert a coordinating conjunction between the two clauses, or separate the clauses into distinct sentences. You can even make one clause dependent upon the other.

Examples: You're going to a concert; you can't wear that.

You're going to a concert, but you can't wear that.

You're going to a concert. You can't wear that.

If you're going to a concert, you can't wear that.

Note that simply removing the comma from a comma splice does not fix the error. Rather, it creates a run-on sentence.

A **sentence fragment** is a collection of words that do not express a complete thought.

Examples: All this year's best peaches.

The long way back to the house.

Including geometry and biology.

To correct a sentence fragment, simply add the parts of the sentence that are missing. If the sentence is missing a subject, add a subject. If the sentence is missing a verb or predicate, add a verb or predicate. In the instance of the last example, a participial phrase, both a subject and a predicate need to be added.

Correct Examples: All this year's best peaches are headed to the grocery stores.

Calvin took the long way back to the house.

Narissa likes all of her classes this year, including geometry and biology.

81

Sentence Structure

Look at these sample questions.

1. Ross was glad he took Megan <u>to prom, they had</u> a lovely time together.

   A. NO CHANGE
   B. to prom, but they had
   C. to prom they had
   D. to prom; they had

The correct answer is D. Answer C is obviously wrong, since some punctuation is necessary. Answer B is correctly punctuated; however, the conjunction *but* is a faulty coordination, making it misleading to the meaning of the sentence.

2. My aunt is an office manager. She is in charge of <u>many tasks, including billing patients, setting appointments, and answering calls</u>.

   F. NO CHANGE
   G. many tasks; including billing patients, setting appointments, and answering calls
   H. many tasks. Including billing patients, setting appointments, and answering calls
   J. many tasks including billing patients setting appointments and answering calls

The best answer is F. Answer G changes the correct comma into an incorrect semicolon. Answer H makes it into a participial phrase fragment. Answer J gets rid of all necessary punctuation altogether. Thus, NO CHANGE is correct.

If you need more practice with sentences and fixing common errors, you could review those sections in your English textbook, ask your teacher for more help, or purchase American Book Company's *Basics Made Easy: Grammar and Usage* book.

Chapter 5

Practice 1: Clauses and Phrases

Directions: Some portions in the following passage have been underlined and numbered. The matching questions offer alternatives for the underlined portion. You can choose one of these, or select NO CHANGE if the original version in the passage is best. If a number appears in a box within the text, the corresponding question will ask about a section of the text that is not underlined (such as a whole paragraph). To choose the best answer for any question, you should read more than just the underlined portion.

The Roots of English

Did you ever think about where English came from? It is part of a language family called Indo-European. At its roots, English is a Germanic language. In the fifth century, tribes from Denmark and northern Germany settled in the British Isles. The Angles, Saxons, and Jutes brought their languages with them. The English language began to take shape.(1) Over time, many other(2) influences on English. The language began to grow and add words from many world cultures, and the three largest language influences(3) were Germanic, Latin, and French. The author and editor Samuel Johnson was also a lexicographer (one who studies words) in 1755 published(4) his *Dictionary of the English Language*. By this time, English was in its modern era.

1. What is the best way to combine these sentences?
   A. As the English language began to take shape, the Angles, Saxons, and Jutes brought their languages with them.
   B. The Angles, Saxons, and Jutes brought their languages with them, and the English language began to take shape.
   C. The English language began to take shape; because the Angles, Saxons, and Jutes brought their languages with them.
   D. The Angles, Saxons, and Jutes brought their languages with them; and the English language began to take shape.

2. F. NO CHANGE
   G. Over time, there were many other
   H. Over time, many other foreign
   J. Over time; many other

Sentence Structure

3. **A.** NO CHANGE

   B. grow and add words from many world cultures; and the three largest language influences

   C. grow, and add words, from many world cultures, the three largest language influences

   D. grow and add words from many world cultures; but the three largest language influences

4. **F.** NO CHANGE

   G. words), in 1755, published

   H. words) in 1755, and published

   J. words) and, in 1755, published

European Languages

Chapter 5

MODIFIERS

A **modifier** is a phrase or clause that helps to clarify the meaning of another word.

Example: Tipping over the trash can, our cat was looking for food.

In this sentence, the phrase *tipping over the trash can* modifies the word *cat*. It describes a condition or tells of a circumstance relevant to the subject. In modern English usage, however, modifiers are frequently misused, leading to them either becoming misplaced or left dangling.

A **misplaced modifier** is a word or phrase that modifies a clause ambiguously; the modifier could possibly apply to either the subject or object of the clause.

Example: Two students competed against the school record diving in the swimming pool.

It is unclear whether the phrase *diving in the swimming pool* describes the students or the school record.

To correct this problem, we place the modifier closer to the word it describes.

Correct Example: Diving in the swimming pool, two students competed against the school record.

A **dangling modifier** is a phrase or clause that comes at the beginning of a sentence but does not modify the subject in the sentence.

Example: Listening to hip hop music, her arms began to move with the rhythm.

The phrase *Listening to hip hop music* modifies the subject *arms*. Since arms cannot listen to music, the phrase *Listening to hip hop music* cannot be the modifier of *arms*.

Correct Example: Listening to hip hop music, Latasha began to move her arms to the rhythm.

Listening to hip hop music correctly describes *Latasha* instead of *arms*.

Other times, a modifier can be ambiguous. If this happens, ask yourself what the author is trying to say. Look at the sentence below.

Example: The silver mine's tour director said <u>when she finished the tour</u> she would take requests for western music.

This sentence can be read in different ways. The sentence needs to be revised based on the author's intent. In a longer passage, the context would most likely determine that intent. The sentence could be revised in two ways. Look carefully at the difference in meaning between the two possible corrections.

Correct Example: The silver mine's tour director said she would take requests for western music <u>when she finished the tour</u>.

Correct Example: <u>When she finished the tour</u>, the silver mine's tour director said she would take requests for western music.

85

Sentence Structure

Take a look at this sample question.

<u>My dog chased a kid down the street on a bicycle.</u>

A. NO CHANGE

B. On a bicycle, my dog chased a kid down the street.

C. My dog chased a kid on a bicycle down the street.

D. My dog chased on a bicycle a kid down the street.

The best answer is C. This question shows a misplaced modifier. Is the dog riding the bicycle, or is the kid riding it? Answers B and D are still unclear if the dog is riding the bicycle. Answer C is the only choice that clearly has the modifier in the correct place.

Practice 2: Modifiers

Directions: Some portions in the following passage have been underlined and numbered. The matching questions offer alternatives for the underlined portion. You can choose one of these, or select NO CHANGE if the original version in the passage is best. If a number appears in a box within the text, the corresponding question will ask about a section of the text that is not underlined (such as a whole paragraph). To choose the best answer for any question, you should read more than just the underlined portion.

The Niagara Falls Stunt

Many foolhardy people have attempted stunts at Niagara Falls, but only one person has been as daring as Charles Blondin. <u>On June 30, 1859, Blondin crossed the Niagara Gorge and lived to tell about it on a tightrope.</u>[1] While halfway across the rope, he paused a moment before completing a backward somersault. <u>Blondin again crossed the Niagara Gorge not only on his tightrope, determined to beat his last performance, but also while riding a bicycle.</u>[2] <u>On August 19, Blondin barely made it, carrying a man on his shoulders, across the gorge.</u>[3] Because it was a challenging stunt, Blondin was forced to stop six times during the crossing so the man on his back could dismount. The Great Blondin had done it again, but this time he had only just made it. <u>Charles Blondin, considered brave or just crazy, will remain a part of history for his many tightrope crossings.</u>[4]

Chapter 5

1. **A.** NO CHANGE
   B. On June 30, 1859, Blondin crossed the Niagara Gorge and lived on a tightrope to tell about it.
   C. On a tightrope, Blondin crossed the Niagara Gorge and lived on June 30, 1859, to tell about it.
   D. On June 30, 1859, Blondin crossed the Niagara Gorge on a tightrope and lived to tell about it.

2. **F.** NO CHANGE
   G. Determined to beat his last performance, Blondin once again crossed the Niagara Gorge not only on his tightrope, but also while riding a bicycle.
   H. Blondin once again crossed the Niagara Gorge not only on his tightrope, but also while riding a bicycle determined to beat his last performance.
   J. Blondin once again, determined to beat his last performance, crossed the Niagara Gorge not only on his tightrope, but also while riding a bicycle.

3. **A.** NO CHANGE
   B. On August 19, across the gorge, Blondin barely made it carrying a man on his shoulders.
   C. On August 19, Blondin, carrying a man on his shoulders, barely made it across the gorge.
   D. On August 19, Blondin barely made it across the gorge, carrying a man on his shoulders.

4. **F.** NO CHANGE
   G. Charles Blondin will remain a part of history, considered brave or just crazy, for his many tightrope crossings.
   H. Charles Blondin considered brave or just crazy a part of history, for his many tightrope crossings.
   J. Charles Blondin will remain a part, considered brave or just crazy, of history for his many tightrope crossings.

Sentence Structure

ERRORS IN CONSTRUCTION

The main purpose of writing is to convey a point to the reader. Sometimes when writing, an author may shift verb tenses or point of view carelessly, leaving the reader lost and confused.

When you are taking the PLAN English Test, you may be asked to revise sentences that have shifts in construction. These errors include shifts in **verb tense** and **person**, as well as **missing or incorrect relative pronouns**.

SHIFTS IN VERB TENSE

The **verb tense** helps readers know when something took place and the relationship of actions of events to one another. It is important to choose one **verb tense** and use it throughout your composition. Although you should change tense to show a particular time relationship, you should not change it without appropriate reason. Remember that verb tenses must match the intended meaning.

> **Correct Shift:** I *remember* when my grandfather *used to take* me out for pancakes when I *visited* him.
>
> **Incorrect Shift:** "The Raven" *contained* repetition that *can help* readers easily memorize it.

SHIFTS IN PERSON

Person refers to the point of view of the writer, as outlined in the chart below.

Point of View		
Person	**Use**	**Pronouns**
first person	the writer speaks	I or we
second person	the writer speaks to the reader	you
third person	the writer speaks about someone or something	he, she, it, or they

Shifts in person have a similar effect on shifts in tense. They can cause confusion by making the reader unsure of the writer's perspective. Consider the following example.

> **Example:** The great thing about pizza is that you can get so many different toppings, so they can all get what we like on it.

Chapter 5

This example changes from second person to third person to first person so quickly that it interferes with the clarity and flow of the sentence. Look at this revision.

Correct Example: The great thing about pizza is that you can get so many different toppings, so you can get what you like on it.

By changing all the pronouns to second person, it is clear the writer is speaking to the reader and explaining what is so great about pizza.

MISSING OR INCORRECT RELATIVE PRONOUNS

As you know, pronouns are words that keep you from having to repeat proper nouns in your writing. A **relative pronoun** acts as a connection in a sentence, relating an adjective clause to the noun or pronoun it modifies.

Examples: People <u>who</u> exercise regularly live longer lives.

The gym, <u>which</u> we had been going to weekly, closed down.

Relative Pronouns		
what	who	whose
whom	which	that

It is important to use relative pronouns when the situation calls for one. However, it is just as important to know which pronoun to use in which scenario. *Who* and *whom* refer only to people, and *which* refers to things and ideas. It is a good rule of thumb that clauses beginning with *that* are normally restrictive and do not need to be separated with commas. Clauses beginning with *which* are usually nonrestrictive and should be separated with commas.

Look at the following sample questions about errors in construction.

1. Larry <u>falls</u> and broke his ankle while practicing the hurdles yesterday.
      A. NO CHANGE   **B.** fell   **C.** will fall   **D.** is falling

The correct answer is B. You must read the sentence as a whole to find that it is written in the past tense. Thus, *fell* is the only possible choice.

2. Mary Ann visited <u>our</u> grandma over her spring break.
      F. NO CHANGE   **G.** their   **H.** its   **J.** her

The correct answer is J. The pronouns shift from the incorrect first person to the correct third person. The answer choices are all in the third person, but the number and voice of answer J is the only correct option.

Sentence Structure

3. I met <u>two candidates attended</u> the interview yesterday.

    A. NO CHANGE

    B. two candidates, that attended

    C. two candidates who attended

    D. two candidates whose attended

The best answer is C. Answer D, *whose*, is not the correct pronoun to use. Answer B is also incorrect; the pronoun *that* is not normally used when referring to people, and it is the incorrect comma usage that makes this a wrong choice.

Practice 3: Errors in Construction

Directions: Some portions in the following passage have been underlined and numbered. The matching questions offer alternatives for the underlined portion. You can choose one of these, or select NO CHANGE if the original version in the passage is best. If a number appears in a box within the text, the corresponding question will ask about a section of the text that is not underlined (such as a whole paragraph). To choose the best answer for any question, you should read more than just the underlined portion.

Writing Effectively for the Web

Writing good content for websites is not as simple as just <u>sitting down and write</u> about the products, business, organization, or so on that the site is devoted to. <u>There are important factors a good copywriter must consider; for instance, you should consider key words. These are words that people on the Internet</u> tend to enter into search engines when researching a topic. If a business or an organization does not use common key words, their site will receive very little traffic. Another factor is the length of the written copy. In general, the shorter and more direct the content, the better. <u>People online tend to be in a hurry and had short attention spans.</u> One glance at a lengthy page of copy and they are liable to feel that it is more than they have time to read, and they move on. <u>Effective copy is copy that can grab the reader's attention quickly, drew him into the site, and then provides them more information as they are interested.</u>

Chapter 5

1. A. NO CHANGE
   B. sit down and write
   C. sitting down and writing
   D. sitting down and written

2. F. NO CHANGE
   G. There are important factors a good copywriter must consider; for instance, they should consider key words.
   H. There are important factors good copywriters must consider; for instance, he should consider key words.
   J. There are important factors a good copywriter must consider; for instance, the writer should consider key words.

3. A. NO CHANGE
   B. These are words, that people on the Internet
   C. These are words which people on the Internet
   D. These are words who people on the Internet

4. F. NO CHANGE
   G. People online tend to be in a hurry and have short attention spans.
   H. People online are tending to be in a hurry and have short attention spans.
   J. People online tended to be in a hurry and have short attention spans.

5. A. NO CHANGE
   B. Effective copy is copy, that can grab the reader's attention quickly, draw them into the site, and then provided them more information as they are interested.
   C. Effective copy is copy that can grab the reader's attention quickly, draw him into the site, and then provide him more information as he is interested.
   D. Effective copy is copy which can grab the reader's attention quickly, draw them into the site, then provides you more information as you are interested.

CHAPTER 5 SUMMARY

An **independent clause** is a group of words that has a subject and predicate and can stand on its own as a sentence.

A **dependent clause** also has a subject and predicate but depends on the main clause.

A **simple sentence** is formed with one independent clause.

When two or more independent clauses are joined, this is a **compound sentence**.

A **complex sentence** is a combination of an independent clause with a dependent clause.

A compound sentence with a dependent clause is a **compound-complex sentence**.

A **run-on sentence**, or a **fused sentence**, is two independent clauses connected without proper punctuation.

Remember, if you are going to use a comma and a conjunction, pick the best conjunction for the meaning of the sentence to avoid **faulty coordination**.

Subordination means one idea is secondary to the other. This means the most important part of the sentence should also be the main part.

Comma splices are punctuation errors in which two independent clauses are joined only by a comma, with no conjunction.

A **sentence fragment** is a collection of words that do not express a complete thought.

Modifiers can be adjectives, adverbs, or phrases or clauses that act as adjectives or adverbs. **Misplaced modifiers** need to be placed near the word(s) they modify and should not be used where they may be ambiguous (possibly modifying words both before and after them). A **dangling modifier** is a word or phrase that modifies a word not clearly stated in the sentence.

Shifts in construction should be avoided so the readers can follow the passage. The common shifts take place with **verb tense** and **person**.

CHAPTER 5 REVIEW

Directions: Some portions in the following passage have been underlined and numbered. The matching questions in the right-hand column offer alternatives for the underlined portion. You can choose one of these, or select NO CHANGE if the original version in the passage is best. If a number appears in a box within the text, the corresponding question will ask about a section of the text that is not underlined (such as a whole paragraph). To choose the best answer for any question, you should read more than just the underlined portion.

A Classic Car Story

[1]

Sterling McCall was in a small Texas town in 1979 while he began collecting cars.
₁

That year, a customer drove a 1927 Ford Model T Doctor's Coupe into McCall's dealership because they wanted to trade it for a new car. The Ford Model T so distinctive and fun to drive, McCall gladly made a deal.
₂ ... ₃

He liked the antique car so much that he decided not to sell it he kept it in a barn on his farm outside of Houston.
₄

1. A. NO CHANGE
   B. Sterling McCall began collecting cars in 1979 in a small Texas town.
   C. In 1979 Sterling McCall lived in a small Texas town, where he began collecting cars.
   D. Sterling McCall lived in 1979 in a small Texas town while collecting cars.

2. F. NO CHANGE
   G. because he wanted to trade it for a new car
   H. because we wanted to trade it for a new car
   J. because it wanted to trade it for a new car

3. A. NO CHANGE
   B. The Ford Model T being so distinctive and fun to drive, McCall's deal.
   C. The Ford Model T was so distinctive and fun to drive, McCall gladly made a deal.
   D. The Ford Model T, so distinctive and fun to drive, gladly made a deal.

4. F. NO CHANGE
   G. he decided not to sell it or he kept it in a barn
   H. he decided not to sell it; and he kept it in a barn
   J. he decided not to sell it, so he kept it in a barn

Sentence Structure

[2]

McCall's hobby of collecting older-model cars became the talk of the town, people began to bring their old cars to the dealership to trade for new cars. In fifteen years, McCall was collecting so many classic and antique cars he has to build garages all over his farm. A 1941 Buick convertible, a 1948 Lincoln Continental convertible, and a 1946 Plymouth convertible were a few of the valuable and rare classics McCall bought, restored, and drove just for fun.

[3]

The collection of cars totaled eighty-eight when McCall finally decided to stop building garages on his farm and open a car museum in Warrenton, a town located three miles from his farm. The Sterling McCall Old Car Museum opened in 1998, which provides a glimpse into the history of the automobile.

5. **A.** NO CHANGE
   B. McCall's hobby of collecting older-model cars became the talk of the town, but people began to bring their old cars to the dealership to trade for new cars.
   C. McCall's hobby of collecting older-model cars became the talk of the town; however, people began to bring their old cars to the dealership to trade for new cars.
   D. McCall's hobby of collecting older-model cars became the talk of the town; people began to bring their old cars to the dealership to trade for new cars.

6. **F.** NO CHANGE
   G. McCall collects so many classic and antique cars he had to build garages all over his farm.
   H. McCall collected so many classic and antique cars he had to build garages all over his farm.
   J. McCall has collected so many classic and antique cars he had to build garages all over his farm.

7. **A.** NO CHANGE
   B. The Sterling McCall Old Car Museum, which provides a glimpse into the history of the automobile, opened in 1998.
   C. The Sterling McCall Old Car Museum, which opened in 1998, which provides a glimpse into the history of the automobile.
   D. The Sterling McCall Old Car Museum opened in 1998, provides a glimpse into the history of the automobile.

Chapter 6
Usage

Usage questions on the PLAN English Test earn points in the following way, ranging from fundamental conventions (up to 15 score points) to sophisticated usage knowledge (28–32 points):

Points	Benchmark Description
13–15	Solve such basic grammatical problems as how to form the past and past participle of irregular but commonly used verbs and how to form comparative and superlative adjectives
16–19	Solve such grammatical problems as whether to use an adverb or adjective form, how to ensure straightforward subject-verb and pronoun-antecedent agreement, and which preposition to use in simple contexts
	Recognize and use the appropriate word in frequently confused pairs such as *there* and *their*, *past* and *passed*, and *led* and *lead*
20–23	Use idiomatically appropriate prepositions, especially in combination with verbs (e.g., *long for*, *appeal to*)
	Ensure that a verb agrees with its subject when there is some text between the two
24–27	Ensure that a pronoun agrees with its antecedent when the two occur in separate clauses or sentences
	Identify the correct past and past participle forms of irregular and infrequently used verbs and form present-perfect verbs by using *have* rather than *of*
28–32	Correctly use reflexive pronouns, the possessive pronouns *its* and *your*, and the relative pronouns *who* and *whom*
	Ensure that a verb agrees with its subject in unusual situations (e.g., when the subject-verb order is inverted or when the subject is an indefinite pronoun)

GRAMMAR AND USAGE

Grammar and usage refers to the way language is used to create effective communication. Standard written English has a complex set of rules and guidelines for correct grammar and usage, which you have been learning for many years in school. This section will help you review some of the rules to keep in mind when you take the PLAN English Test.

Usage

VERBS

A **verb** is a word that expresses a physical action (*run, jump, read*) or mental action (*think, know, believe*). Verbs also express a state of being (*is, are, appears*). Verbs describe what the sentence subject is doing or being.

There is much to be said about verbs. A sentence must contain a verb to be a complete thought. In the case of an imperative command, a sentence may consist of a single verb, as in "Stop!" There are different verb **forms** and **tenses**, but every verb is essential to the meaning of a sentence.

Understanding verbs in all their forms and usages is an important skill to have when you take the PLAN English Test. Some questions on the test might ask you to choose the right form of a verb or to ensure a verb agrees with its subject. First, let's look at the different forms of verbs.

There are three types of verbs: **action**, **linking**, and **helping**.

An **action verb** tells that something is happening, has happened, or will happen. It can show a physical or mental action.

> **Examples:** The cat *clawed* at the screen.
>
> Apparently, she *wants* to come inside.
>
> She *will run* all around the house now.

A **linking verb** connects the subject with a word or words that describe it, such as predicate nouns or adjectives. Linking verbs also can be used to express a state of being.

> **Examples:** The cat's fur *feels* soft.
>
> The cat *is* a domesticated animal.

A **helping verb** is a word or group of words that joins with a main verb to help the meaning by creating a verb phrase. A **verb phrase** is a group of words working together to act as the verb.

> **Examples:** The cat *has scratched* the furniture before.
>
> We *could have removed* her claws.
>
> The procedure *would hurt* her too much.

Sometimes parts of the verb phrase are separated. The words that come between them are not part of the verb.

> **Examples:** My mother *has* never *liked* cats.
>
> *Do* you *own* a cat?

Chapter 6

VERB TENSES

In addition to verb forms, the various verb tenses are also important to keep in mind. **Verb tense** shows the time of an action or condition. The surrounding words in a sentence and the intent behind the sentence meaning will indicate which tense a verb should take. Let's review the most commonly used tenses.

Present tense is used to express action that is happening now, or an action that happens continually or regularly.

> **Example:** He *walks* to school every day.

Past tense is used to express action that has already happened.

> **Example:** He *walked* to school last year.

Future tense is used to express action that will happen in the future.

> **Example:** He *will walk* to school next year.

Present perfect tense is used to express an action that began in the past but continues in the present or is completed in the present.

> **Example:** He *has walked* to school since kindergarten.

Past perfect tense is used to express an action in the past that happened before another past action.

> **Example:** His father *had walked* to school as a boy.

Future perfect tense is used to express an action that will begin in the future and will be completed by a certain time beyond then.

> **Example:** He *will have walked* many miles by the time he graduates.

Note: As stated above, when using the perfect tense, the verb *to have* is used. One common error that has emerged over time is the incorrect use of the word *of* instead of *have*.

> **Incorrect Example:** I *should of called* to tell you I was running late.

The word *of* should never be used in place of *have* in the perfect tense.

> **Correct Example:** I *should have called* to tell you I was running late.

You will notice that some tenses use a **participle**. A participle is a verb that ends with *-ing*, *-ed*, or *-en*. Used alone, these verbs can act as adjectives or nouns in a sentence. Examples include "Your redecorated room looks great" (*redecorated* is used as an adjective) and "I love traveling" (*traveling* is used as a noun). But when used with helping verbs, participles form the perfect tenses.

Usage

IRREGULAR VERBS

Verbs have different tenses. Most verbs in English form tenses in the same way. For example, the verb *walk* is in the present tense. To form the past tense of *walk*, add an *-ed* to make it *walked*. The verb *walk* is a regular verb.

Other verbs are irregular. Different tenses of these verbs are not formed the same way regular verbs are formed. Think of the verb *run*. Doubling the last consonant and adding an *-ed* to make the word *runned* is incorrect. Instead, the past tense of *run* is *ran*.

Irregular verbs do not follow a format, so readers and writers must memorize the different tenses of irregular verbs. Notice that some of these irregular verbs have two ways of spelling the past tense and/or past participle; sometimes these have slightly different meanings. If you are not sure which form to use correctly, look them both up in the dictionary.

Some Common Irregular Verbs					
Present Tense	**Past Tense**	**Past Participle**	**Present Tense**	**Past Tense**	**Past Participle**
arise	arose	arisen	keep	kept	kept
be	was/were	been	know	knew	known
begin	began	begun	lay	laid	laid
bite	bit	bitten/bit	lie	lay	lain
break	broke	broken	lose	lost	lost
catch	caught	caught	prove	proved	proved
choose	chose	chosen	ride	rode	ridden
dive	dived/dove	dived/dove	see	saw	seen
do	did	done	sing	sang	sung
dream	dreamed/dreamt	dreamt	speak	spoke	spoken
eat	ate	eaten	swim	swam	swum
fly	flew	flown	take	took	taken
get	got	gotten	tear	tore	torn
give	gave	given	wear	wore	worn
go	went	gone	write	wrote	written

The **present participle** is used when a writer wants to point out an action that is continuous, was continuous, or will be continuous or in progress. The present participle is formed by adding *-ing* to a verb.

> **Example 1:** I *was being* my usual self at the party. (The action has been continuous.)
>
> **Example 2:** He *is studying* for his medical exam. (The action is continuous.)
>
> **Example 3:** She *will be working* as a nurse. (The action will be continuous.)

The **past participle** is used when an action has been completed. Some form of *be* or *have* must be used with a past participle to form a complete verb in a sentence.

> **Examples:** Da Vinci *had worked* hard on the *Mona Lisa*.
>
> I *have been* attending this school for two years.

SUBJECT-VERB AGREEMENT

In any given passage, everything must agree. In **subject-verb agreement**, if the subject is singular, the verb must be singular; if the subject is plural, the verb must be plural.

Undoubtedly, you have learned to conjugate most regular and irregular verbs at some time in school. However, there can be some tricky cases.

> **Example 1, simple agreement:**
>
> The dog *barks* loudly.
>
> Her cousins *listen* intently.
>
> **Example 2, compound singular subjects:**
>
> Josh and Davey *want* some ice cream
>
> Neither Mrs. Rampling nor I *want* to go.

(A conjunction like *or* or *nor* separates the subjects—unlike *and*, which joins them so that they do not become plural.)

> **Example 3, subject separated from verb:** A bushel of apples *is keeping* the doctor from our door.
>
> **Example 4, collective nouns:** The jury *deliberates* on the verdict. (acting as a group)
>
> Sometimes the jury *disagree*, and a verdict cannot be reached. (acting as individuals)

Usage

Example 5, indefinite pronouns: Of the two choices, neither (choice) *appeals* much to me.

Both (choices) *are* rather unpleasant.

Example 6, inverted subject-verb order: Under the bed *are* boxes filled with memories.

Look at some sample questions.

1. Matthew <u>will swimming</u> lead in the relay next week.

   A. NO CHANGE   **B.** has swum   **C.** swam   **D.** will swim

The correct answer is D. Since the sentence is talking about an event that occurs in the future, the verb needs to be in future tense.

2. Carl and Rahul <u>studies</u> hard for their tests.

   F. NO CHANGE   **G.** studying   **H.** study   **J.** are studied

The correct answer is H. Since the sentence contains a compound subject, the verb needs to agree in number. Answers G and J are the wrong forms of the verb *study* and therefore are not correct.

Gone <u>is</u> the days of VCRs and cassette tapes.

   A. NO CHANGE   **B.** are   **C.** were   **D.** be

The correct answer is B. The inverted order might confuse you, but the sentence's subject is actually *days*; therefore, the correct agreement would be the verb *are*.

Practice 1: Verbs

Directions: Some portions in the following passage have been underlined and numbered. The matching questions offer alternatives for the underlined portion. You can choose one of these, or select NO CHANGE if the original version in the passage is best. If a number appears in a box within the text, the corresponding question will ask about a section of the text that is not underlined (such as a whole paragraph). To choose the best answer for any question, you should read more than just the underlined portion.

Most of us <u>has been going</u> to the pool since we were young, and we know that the lifeguard
             1

on duty monitors the swimmers to make sure they are safe. Most lifeguards <u>have swam</u> on swim
                                                                            2

teams for years, so they are expert swimmers and physically fit. A lifeguard's job can be

extremely dull, but it also <u>include</u> moments of excitement or terror. For instance, if a
                             3

100

Chapter 6

young child <u>felled</u> into the deep end, the lifeguard must be paying attention and respond quickly
⁴
to save the child from drowning. Sometimes older kids dislike the rules enforced by the

lifeguard; however, the lifeguard and pool manager <u>sets</u> the rules to prevent accidents and
⁵
injuries from occurring. One time a swimmer had a spinal injury and had to go to the hospital.

He <u>should of listened</u> to the lifeguard and not dived into the shallow end of the pool. Remember
⁶
that neither your coach nor the lifeguard <u>want</u> you to have an accident.
⁷

1.   A. NO CHANGE   C. have been going
      B. has gone   D. go

2.   F. NO CHANGE   H. have swum
      G. have swimmed   J. have swimming

3.   A. NO CHANGE   C. has included
      B. included   D. includes

4.   F. NO CHANGE   H. fells
      G. fall   J. falls

5.   A. NO CHANGE   C. set
      B. setted   D. sat

6.   F. NO CHANGE   H. should have listened
      G. should listened   J. should listen

7.   A. NO CHANGE   C. wanted
      B. wants   D. have wanted

Usage

PRONOUNS

Pronouns take the place of nouns. The noun that the pronoun replaces is called the *antecedent*. There are three **cases** of pronouns. For example, if the antecedent is *Joe*, three pronoun forms might fit, depending on the context: *he, him,* or *his*.

Nominative pronouns are used whenever a pronoun is in the place of a subject.

>**Example:** Amy and *I* are both reading the same book.

Objective pronouns are used when the pronoun answers the questions "What?" or "Whom?" after the action verb.

>**Example:** Nathan heard *him* give an excellent speech.

Possessive pronouns are used to show ownership or attachment.

>**Example:** The authors provide *their* credentials in the book's preface.

Consider how the pronoun is used in the sentence to determine the correct form. For quick and easy reference, this table will help you review pronoun cases.

Personal Pronoun Forms		
Nominative	**Objective**	**Possessive**
I	me	my, mine
you	you	your, yours
she	her	her, hers
he	him	his
it	it	its
we	us	our, ours
they	them	their, theirs
who	whom	whose
whoever	whomever	whosever

It's helpful to remember that a possessive pronoun never takes an apostrophe. *Its* and *your* are often confused with *it's* and *you're*. A trick is to insert "it is" or "you are/were" in the sentence to see if it makes sense. If not, then use the possessive pronouns *its* or *your*.

Examples: The bird layered its nest with twigs. (*It is* doesn't work.)

The captain thinks it's (it is) going to storm.

We can tell you're (you are) busy.

Take your jacket because it is cold outside. (*You are* doesn't fit.)

REFLEXIVE PRONOUNS

Reflexive pronouns are used when the object of the sentence is the same as the subject. Each personal pronoun has a corresponding reflexive pronoun.

Reflexive Pronouns			
Personal Pronoun	**Reflexive Pronoun**	**Personal Pronoun**	**Reflexive Pronoun**
I	myself	you	yourself/yourselves
me	myself	he	himself
she	herself	it	itself
they	themselves	we	ourselves

Reflexive pronouns are used in three cases:
- when the subject and object of a sentence are the same
- as the object of a preposition, again when the subject and object are the same
- to emphasize the subject

Here are some examples.

Examples: Mina treated *herself* to an ice cream sundae after a hard day's work.

We saw the evidence for *ourselves*.

Bobby and Jean tied their shoelaces *themselves*.

Usage

RELATIVE PRONOUNS

Relative pronouns like *who, whom, that, which,* and *whose* begin **relative clauses**. Relative clauses are dependent clauses that modify a person, thing, or idea in the independent clause.

> **Examples:** The movie *that* I saw last night was scary.
>
> I donated my blue jeans, *which* were gently used, to the clothes drive.

People commonly confuse *who* and *whom*. *Who* refers to the subject of the clause, the person doing the action. *Whom* refers to the object of the clause, the person receiving the action.

> **Examples:** People *who* talk on their cellphones at the movies annoy me.
>
> The woman to *whom* I spoke had a thick New England accent.

In the first example, *who* is the subject of the dependent clause *who talk on their cellphones*, which modifies the antecedent *people*. In the second example, *whom* is the object of the clause *to whom I spoke*, which modifies the antecedent *woman*. The woman is being spoken to, not doing the speaking. Remember that *whom* usually follows a preposition, like *to, for,* or *at*.

Also, be aware that clauses beginning with *that* do not use a comma, but clauses beginning with *which* do.

PRONOUN AGREEMENT

Pronoun-antecedent agreement is absolutely necessary for understanding common sentences. Every pronoun used must have an antecedent to which it refers. Here are some rules to remember when working on agreement.

- When a sentence has **compound antecedents** joined with *and*, the pronoun must be plural.
- Having pronouns agree with **indefinite-pronoun antecedents** mostly depends on the logic of the text. Some indefinite pronouns like *one* will always take the singular pronoun, while some indefinite pronouns like *several* always take the plural pronoun.
- Sometimes an antecedent will not be present in the clause or sentence where a pronoun is featured. If the antecedent is in another clause or sentence, make sure it is clear which antecedent is meant. This will avoid **vague pronoun reference**.
- Remember that sometimes the antecedent appears after the pronoun.
- A pronoun must also agree with its antecedent in **gender**.

> **Incorrect Examples:** Daniel and James left *his* homework at home.
>
> One of the horses threw *their* shoe during the race.
>
> Ron taught Kylie how to draw, and *they* picked it up very quickly.
>
> **Correct Examples:** Daniel and James left *their* homework at home.
>
> One of the horses threw *its* shoe during the race.
>
> Ron taught Kylie how to draw, and *she* picked it up very quickly.

Chapter 6

Amanda left her lunch box at school.
In this sentence, *her* is a pronoun. It takes the place of the name *Amanda*.

The students lined up to wait for their PE teacher.
In this sentence, *their* is a pronoun. It takes the place of *students*.

The school celebrated its 50th year.
In this sentence, *its* is a pronoun. It takes the place of the word *school*.

Pronouns

Let's look at some sample questions.

1. The <u>house that my uncle wants to buy</u> is too expensive.

   A. NO CHANGE
   B. house, that my uncle wants to buy
   C. house which my uncle wants to buy
   D. house whom my uncle wants to buy

The correct answer is A. The relative pronoun *that* is correctly used and punctuated. Answer D is obviously wrong because *whom* would not refer to *house*. Answers B and C are incorrect because they are not punctuated properly.

Usage

2. Maggie and Layla got <u>her</u> toenails painted at a salon yesterday.

    F. NO CHANGE   **G.** them   **H.** its   **J.** their

The correct choice is answer J. Since the subject is plural, the pronoun must also be plural.

Practice 2: Pronouns and Agreement

Directions: Some portions in the following passage have been underlined and numbered. The matching questions offer alternatives for the underlined portion. You can choose one of these, or select NO CHANGE if the original version in the passage is best. If a number appears in a box within the text, the corresponding question will ask about a section of the text that is not underlined (such as a whole paragraph). To choose the best answer for any question, you should read more than just the underlined portion.

    Household pets such as cats and dogs can bring families a lot of joy. While many people prefer one or the other, I think that both cats and dogs make excellent family pets. Cats and dogs are very playful, especially when <u>it is</u> kittens and puppies. <u>She provides her owners</u> with
                                                1   2
endless entertainment, performing silly tricks and setting off on many household adventures. Cats and dogs also bond with family members, seeking out attention and affection from their human companions. Most families with cats and dogs find that <u>his</u> pets make <u>them</u> smile every
                                                        3   4
day.

1.   **A.** NO CHANGE   **C.** they are
       B. he is   **D.** I am

2.   **F.** NO CHANGE   **H.** They provide your owners
       G. We provide our owners   **J.** They provide their owners

3.   **A.** NO CHANGE   **C.** your
       B. their   **D.** my

4.   **F.** NO CHANGE   **H.** we
       G. us   **J.** her

Chapter 6

ADJECTIVES AND ADVERBS

Adjectives are words that modify or describe nouns and pronouns. Adjectives answer the following questions:

- Which?
- How many?
- What kind?

In contrast to many other languages, English almost always places adjectives before the word or words that they modify.

> **Examples:** Snow White lived with *seven* dwarves. (*Seven* modifies the noun *dwarves*.)
>
> Roberta avoids checking her mailbox on *rainy* days. (*Rainy* modifies the noun *days*.)

Adverbs are used to modify many different kinds of words. Adverbs can modify verbs, adjectives, or other adverbs. Frequently, adverbs end in *-ly*, but this is not always true. All adverbs answer one of these questions:

- Where?
- When?
- In what manner?
- To what extent?

> **Examples:** Carlos ate the candy *slowly*. (*Slowly* modifies the verb *ate*.)
>
> *Extremely* anxious about the test, Fiona crammed all night. (*Extremely* modifies the adjective *anxious*.)

The best way to decide whether to use an adjective or an adverb is to ask yourself what type of word you are describing. Adjectives modify only nouns and pronouns; adverbs modify verbs, adjectives, and other adverbs.

COMPARATIVE AND SUPERLATIVE MODIFIERS

Comparative and **superlative** modifiers are used when comparing items to each other. These adjectives and adverbs "weigh" the differences between two or more things.

Comparative modifiers compare one thing to another. They commonly end in *-er* or use *less* or *more* in front of the modifier.

> **Examples:** My Halloween candy pile is *bigger* than my sister's.
>
> Duncan has become *more experienced* in his field.

107

Usage

Superlative modifiers compare one thing to everything else. They commonly use *-est*, *least*, or *most* in a sentence.

> **Examples:** Martha lives in the *tallest* building on the street.
>
> Getting his blood drawn is Scott's *least favorite* part of the physical exam.

When deciding which form of the modifier should be used, remember that a **one-syllable word** uses the *-er* or *-est* form. In the case of **two-syllable words**, most also use *more* or *less* and *most* or *least*, but some behave like one-syllable words (*easier*, not *more easy*; *simpler*, not *more simple*). For some two-syllable words, either rule is acceptable (*more clever* and *cleverer* are both correct; *quieter* and *more quiet* are both correct). **Three-syllable words** use *more* or *less* and *most* or *least*. Never use the *-er* ending with *more* or *less*, and do not use the *-est* ending with *most* or *least*. Use one or the other.

Remember that there also are **irregular modifiers** that follow none of the rules above but rather change spelling in their comparative and superlative forms. Examples are featured in the table below.

Modifier	Comparative Form	Superlative Form
good	better	best
bad	worse	worst
far	farther/further	farthest/furthest
little	less	least
much/many	more	most

Look at some sample questions.

1. Eugene thinks he is the <u>smarter</u> person in the whole tenth grade.

   A. NO CHANGE
   B. smartest
   C. more smart
   D. most smart

The correct answer is B. The original wording is not correct because most likely there are more than two people in the entire tenth grade to compare. Answers C and D are incorrect because one-syllable modifiers take an *-er* or *-est* ending.

Chapter 6

2. My sister has <u>more beautifuler</u> hair than I do.

F. NO CHANGE

G. beautifuler

H. the most beautiful

J. more beautiful

The correct answer is J. Answer G is not correct because three-syllable superlative words need to use *most* or *least* with the adjective or adverb without adding an *-er*. Although it is properly formed, H is not correct because the sentence is only comparing two people, meaning it should use the comparative form.

PREPOSITIONS

A **preposition** is a word in a sentence that shows the relationship in space (position) or time between nouns, pronouns, and other words in a sentence. A preposition is followed by a noun or pronoun, which is the **object of the preposition**. The preposition and object of the preposition together make up the **prepositional phrase**.

> **Examples:** Ruth cashed her check *at* the last bank window. (*At* is the preposition, and *window* is the object of the preposition. The prepositional phrase is *at the last bank window*.)
>
> Our cousins will be arriving *on* a Greyhound bus. (*On* is the preposition, and *bus* is the object of the preposition. The prepositional phrase is *on a Greyhound bus*.)

Idioms are common expressions used in a specific language that may not mean the same as their literal definitions. Often, idioms use prepositions in their wording. These prepositions must be idiomatically appropriate, especially when they're combined with certain verbs.

> **Examples:** I don't *cotton to* such harsh methods. (The phrase *cotton for* would be incorrect.)
>
> It's rude to *talk down* to someone who's different than you are. (The phrase *talk under* would not be correct.)
>
> Jarrell was *at a loss* for words when Margo dumped her spaghetti on his head. (The phrase *in a loss* would not be correct.)

Remember that some idioms are followed by specific prepositions. Can you think of any more idiomatic phrases that use prepositions?

Usage

Practice 3: Adjectives, Adverbs, and Prepositions

Directions: Some portions in the following passage have been underlined and numbered. The matching questions offer alternatives for the underlined portion. You can choose one of these, or select NO CHANGE if the original version in the passage is best. If a number appears in a box within the text, the corresponding question will ask about a section of the text that is not underlined (such as a whole paragraph). To choose the best answer for any question, you should read more than just the underlined portion.

The Folly of Fast Food

Health experts agree that fast food can be <u>direct</u> linked to the disturbing increase in obesity <u>to</u> the United States today. More and more Americans are pulling up to the drive-through every day. The fact that McDonald's and other chains offer <u>cheaply</u> and convenient meals <u>appeals for</u> Americans. Many people claim to be too busy to prepare our own food at home. They continue ordering artery-clogging foods and opting for the "biggie" fries and soda—<u>willful endangeringly</u> their health with every trip. It is common knowledge that fast food will lead to obesity and a slew of other health problems. Still, Americans continue to visit fast food restaurants in record numbers. What Americans don't seem to realize is that they're gambling <u>without</u> their lives each time they pull up to the window.

1. A. NO CHANGE B. directer C. directly D. directs

2. F. NO CHANGE G. in H. at J. without

3. A. NO CHANGE B. cheaper C. cheapest D. cheap

4. F. NO CHANGE G. appeals to H. appeals at J. appeals in

5. A. NO CHANGE
    B. willful endanger
    C. willfully endangering
    D. willfully endangerly

6. F. NO CHANGE G. by H. between J. with

FREQUENTLY CONFUSED WORD PAIRS

Some word pairs frequently are confused because they sound or look similar; they're called **homonyms**. Because they have different meanings, it's important to know which word is correct depending on the context of the sentence.

Here are some other frequently confused word pairs that you will commonly see.

Common Homonyms				
affect:	noun: emotion or feeling	**to:**	in the direction of
	verb: to produce a change in	**too:**	as well, besides, also
effect:	noun: result	**two:**	one more than one
	verb: to bring about		
		wear:	to have on the body
accept:	to willingly receive	**were:**	past tense of *be*
except:	left out	**we're:**	contraction of *we are*
		where:	location
its:	possessive form of *it*	**weather:**	atmospheric conditions
it's:	contraction of *it has* or *it is*	**whether:**	if
right:	true; opposite of left	**who's:**	contraction of *who is* or *who has*
rite:	a solemn act	**whose:**	possessive form of *who*
write:	to form or inscribe on a surface		
		your:	possessive form of *you*
their:	possessive form of *they*	**you're:**	contraction of *you are*
there:	in that place		
they're:	contraction of *they are*		**continued on next page**

Usage

personal:	private or individual	**cents:**	1/100 of a dollar
personnel:	employees	**sense:**	verb: to feel or experience
			noun: a feeling
plain:	flat stretch of land; easy to discern perception		
plane:	airplane; flat surface	**advice:**	suggestion
		advise:	to suggest
bear:	noun: a large, heavy mammal	**one:**	the first whole number
	verb: to suffer or endure	**won:**	to have gained; to have had success over others
bare:	without covering, naked		
counsel:	advice, to advise	**threw:**	past tense of *throw*
council:	leadership group	**through:**	into and out again
passed:	the past participle of *to pass*	**led:**	past tense and past participle form of the verb *to lead*
past:	a point in time or space that has already occurred	**lead:**	the element on the periodic table (When pronounced like "leed," *lead* means to show the way.)

Look at the following sample questions.

1. "She doesn't have much common <u>cents</u>, does she?" Isla's dad laughed, after watching the new puppy run into the chair leg again.

    A. NO CHANGE
    B. scents
    C. sense
    D. since

The correct answer is C. The original wording is not correct because *cents* means "parts of a dollar." B is not correct because *scents* means "aromas," and D is not correct because *since* means "from one time to another."

Chapter 6

2. We're going to California next summer.

    F. NO CHANGE   **G.** too   **H.** two   **J.** tow

The correct answer is F, NO CHANGE. Answer G is not correct because *too* means "also." H is incorrect because *two* is a number, and J is incorrect because *tow* means "to pull an object" and is not pronounced the same way as *to*, *too*, or *two*.

Practice 4: Frequently Confused Word Pairs

Directions: Some portions in the following passage have been underlined and numbered. The matching questions offer alternatives for the underlined portion. You can choose one of these, or select NO CHANGE if the original version in the passage is best. If a number appears in a box within the text, the corresponding question will ask about a section of the text that is not underlined (such as a whole paragraph). To choose the best answer for any question, you should read more than just the underlined portion.

Trudy poured over her advanced chemistry notes; she had a big exam tomorrow, and she
       1

really had to study hard. She barely past her last test, just scraping by with a D minus. Trudy
                            2

sighed anxiously, thinking about the upcoming meeting with her guidance counselor. She

hoped the counselor would be able to advice her on which colleges to visit over the winter
                                  3

break. This chemistry exam could have a huge effect on her final grade. If she was ever going
                              4

to become a lab technician, she needed to have top marks in all her science courses. Trudy took

a deep breath and said allowed, "You can do this." She was confident because there had been
               5

times when her hard work had lead to success.
             6

1.   **A.** NO CHANGE   **B.** pour   **C.** pored   **D.** pores

2.   **F.** NO CHANGE   **G.** passed   **H.** pasted   **J.** pass

3.   **A.** NO CHANGE   **B.** advices   **C.** advised   **D.** advise

4.   **F.** NO CHANGE   **G.** affect   **H.** effected   **J.** affects

5.   **A.** NO CHANGE   **B.** allow   **C.** allowance   **D.** aloud

6.   F. NO CHANGE   G. leaded   H. led   J. leaden

CHAPTER 6 SUMMARY

A **verb** is a word that expresses a physical action or mental state of being.

There are three types of verbs: **action**, **linking**, and **helping**.

Verb tense shows the time of an action or condition.

The **present** and **past participles** of **irregular verbs** are not formed the same way regular verbs are formed.

In **subject-verb agreement**, if the subject is singular, the verb must be singular; if the subject is plural, the verb must be plural.

Pronouns take the place of nouns. There are three **cases** of pronouns: **nominative**, **objective**, and **possessive**.

Reflexive pronouns are used when the object of the sentence is the same as the subject.

Relative pronouns like *who, whom, that, which,* and *whose* begin **relative clauses**. Relative clauses are dependent clauses that modify a person, thing, or idea in the independent clause.

Each **pronoun** must agree in tense with the **antecedent** to which it refers.

Adjectives are words that modify or describe nouns and pronouns.

Adverbs are words that modify verbs, adjectives, or other adverbs.

Comparative and **superlative** modifiers are used when comparing items to each other.

A **preposition** is a word in a sentence that shows the relationship in space (position) or time between nouns, pronouns, and other words in a sentence.

Prepositions must be **idiomatically appropriate** when they are combined with verbs in phrases like *appeal to* and *long for*.

Homonyms are **frequently confused word pairs** that sound or look similar, like *there/their*, *led/lead*, and *passed/past*.

CHAPTER 6 REVIEW

Directions: Some portions in the following passage have been underlined and numbered. The matching questions in the right-hand column offer alternatives for the underlined portion. You can choose one of these, or select NO CHANGE if the original version in the passage is best. If a number appears in a box within the text, the corresponding question will ask about a section of the text that is not underlined (such as a whole paragraph). To choose the best answer for any question, you should read more than just the underlined portion.

Richard was always trying to compete with his older brother, Chris, because he felt like Chris got all the attention from <u>there</u>
1
parents and teachers. Whenever Richard said something funny in class to try to get laughs, his teacher would <u>jump down his throat</u>;
2
however, she always praised Chris for being so witty and clever. Richard <u>should of knew</u>
3
his teacher, <u>who</u> he didn't like, would treat
4
him <u>unfair</u>. His parents also <u>acts</u> like Chris
5 6

1. **A.** NO CHANGE
   B. they're
   C. their
   D. they are

2. **F.** NO CHANGE
   G. scold him
   H. make him cry
   J. attack him

3. **A.** NO CHANGE
   B. should have known
   C. should of known
   D. should of know

4. **F.** NO CHANGE
   G. whose
   H. whom
   J. who've

5. **A.** NO CHANGE
   B. unfairily
   C. unfairy
   D. unfairly

6. **F.** NO CHANGE
   G. acted
   H. has acted
   J. acting

Usage

was <u>smarter</u>. At the <u>passed</u> Fourth of July
     7   8
picnic, their father told a friend that Chris

<u>have been reading</u> since he was three.
        9
Richard wished his dad would brag about

how Richard hit the ball the <u>farther</u> at his last
                          10

baseball game. He <u>had never before seen</u> a
                        11

ball fly so far. Richard told <u>myself</u> he was an
                      12
amazing ball player, but he wanted his

7. **A.** NO CHANGE
   B. smart
   C. smartest
   D. most smart

8. **F.** NO CHANGE
   G. pasted
   H. past
   J. pasts

9. **A.** NO CHANGE
   B. has reading
   C. have read
   D. had been reading

10. **F.** NO CHANGE
    G. farthest
    H. far
    J. furthest

11. **A.** NO CHANGE
    B. has never before seen
    C. have never before seen
    D. had never saw

12. **F.** NO CHANGE
    G. themselves
    H. himself
    J. herself

parents to say it. Neither <u>appreciate</u> his
                            13

talents. This fact <u>lead</u> Richard to believe their
                    14

favorite son <u>was</u> Chris. Richard longed for his
              15

parents' approval. <u>How else should you feel
                    16
when your not you're parents' favorite child?</u>

13. A. NO CHANGE
    B. appreciated
    C. appreciating
    D. have appreciated

14. F. NO CHANGE
    G. leads
    H. leaded
    J. led

15. A. NO CHANGE
    B. were
    C. was being
    D. are

16. F. NO CHANGE
    G. How else should you feel when you're not you're parents' favorite child?
    H. How else should you feel when your not your parents' favorite child?
    J. How else should you feel when you're not your parents' favorite child?

Usage

Chapter 7
Punctuation

Punctuation questions on the PLAN English Test earn points in the following way, ranging from fundamental punctuation knowledge (up to 15 score points) to sophisticated punctuation knowledge (28–32 points):

Points	Benchmark Description
13–15	Delete commas that create basic sense problems (e.g., between verb and direct object)
16–19	Provide appropriate punctuation in straightforward situations (e.g., items in a series)
	Delete commas that disturb the sentence flow (e.g., between modifier and modified element)
20–23	Use commas to set off simple parenthetical phrases
	Delete unnecessary commas when an incorrect reading of the sentence suggests a pause that should be punctuated (e.g., between verb and direct object clause)
24–27	Use punctuation to set off complex parenthetical phrases
	Recognize and delete unnecessary commas based on a careful reading of a complicated sentence (e.g., between the elements of a compound subject or compound verb joined by *and*)
	Use apostrophes to indicate simple possessive nouns
	Recognize inappropriate uses of colons and semicolons
28–32	Use commas to set off a nonessential/nonrestrictive appositive or clause
	Deal with multiple punctuation problems (e.g., compound sentences containing unnecessary commas and phrases that may or may not be parenthetical)
	Use an apostrophe to show possession, especially with irregular plural nouns
	Use a semicolon to indicate a relationship between closely related independent clauses

This chapter reviews what you have learned about **punctuation** rules. As with the grammar and usage chapter, the punctuation chapter is not meant to teach you any new concepts. Its purpose is to review what you already know and give you practice in skills that will be tested on the PLAN English Test.

Punctuation

END PUNCTUATION

As you have learned, **end punctuation** helps a reader to understand sentences. When you know what a sentence is saying, you know what type of end punctuation is supposed to be there; however, when you are reading something new, you may not get the full meaning of what is written if a sentence does not have proper end punctuation.

The three common punctuation marks for ending sentences are as follows:

A **period** comes after a complete statement.

A **question mark** comes after any question.

An **exclamation point** follows an emotional or forceful statement.

Practice 1: End Punctuation

Directions: For each sentence, choose the best end punctuation mark for the place indicated by a number.

"Why are we here today (1)" asked Coach Roberts.

"Because we're winners (2)" shouted Marty, the team captain.

"That's right!" Coach Roberts agreed. "We have worked too hard this season to give up now. No matter what the score ends up being out there today, remember you are all winners (3) Now, get out there, and let's play some football!"

"Yeah(4)" exclaimed the rest of the team.

1.
   A. NO CHANGE   B. .   C. ?   D. !

2.
   F. NO CHANGE   G. .   H. ?   J. !

3.
   A. NO CHANGE   B. .   C. ?   D. !

4.
   F. NO CHANGE   G. .   H. ?   J. !

Chapter 7

INTERNAL PUNCTUATION

On the PLAN English Test, questions that test **internal punctuation** will focus on the relationship of punctuation to meaning. For example, you will want to focus on properly joining phrases and clauses, avoiding ambiguity, and indicating appositives.

COMMAS

Much of internal punctuation involves using **commas**.

Commas are used to set off phrases and clauses, such as adjective clauses, dependent clauses, and independent clauses (with a conjunction).

Example: Gino played basketball last year, but he decided to try out for the football team this year.

Commas are used to set off items in a series. (Note: There is much debate about whether to insert the final comma before the conjunction in a list. Ask your teacher which format he or she prefers you use.)

Example: Tara bought a pair of shoes, a new purse, a sequined dress, and three bottles of nail polish on her shopping spree yesterday.

Remember this tip:

To determine when you use commas with items in a series, follow the *and* rule. Insert *and* between adjectives, verbs, adverbs, or nouns. If the sentence makes sense with *and*, then the items in the series are coordinate and can be separated by commas. Otherwise, they are not separated by commas.

Example: The principal found an updated Atlanta telephone book.

(In this case, the sentence does not make sense with *and* inserted, so the adjectives are not separated by commas.)

Example: The principal is fair, friendly, and tolerant.

(In this case, the sentence makes sense with *and* inserted between the adjectives, so they can be separated by commas.)

Commas are used to set off appositives. **Appositives** are words, phrases, or clauses that mean the same thing as or further explain a noun or pronoun in a sentence.

Example: Elizabeth Taylor, famously known for her role as Cleopatra, died on March 23, 2011.

Punctuation

Commas are used to set off nonrestrictive elements from the rest of the sentence. **Nonrestrictive elements** are clauses, appositives, and phrases that are not essential to the meaning of the sentence and the words they modify.

> **Example:** *The Hurt Locker*, an award-winning picture, grossed over $17 million at the box office during its run.

On the other hand, **restrictive elements** are essential to the meaning of the sentence and the words they modify and are *not* set off by commas. (Note: Clauses beginning with *that* are never set off with commas.)

> **Example:** The fruit that fell out of those trees is bruised.

Commas are used to set off parenthetical phrases from the rest of the sentence.

> **Example:** The house on the corner, in my opinion, has the cleanest yard on the block.

Transitional expressions such as conjunctive adverbs are also set off with commas.

> **Example:** My records, however, indicate that he paid his taxes every year.

Commas usually follow an introductory word or phrase.

> **Examples:** Besides, everything we needed was right there.
>
> When I drive home from school, I go right by your house.

It is important to know these comma rules—and it is just as important to know when *not* to use a comma.

Never use commas between modifiers and the word they modify.

> **Incorrect Example:** Reba gave me a red, scarf for Christmas. (There is no comma needed between *red* and *scarf*.)
>
> **Correct Example:** Reba gave me a red scarf for Christmas.

Never use commas between a verb and the direct object clause.

> **Incorrect Example:** Let's read, *The Red Badge of Courage* today. (There is no comma needed after the verb *read*.)
>
> **Correct Example:** Let's read *The Red Badge of Courage* today.

Never use commas after coordinating conjunctions that only connect words or phrases.

> **Incorrect Example:** I have a cat, and a dog. (There is no comma needed after *cat*.)
>
> **Correct Example:** I have a cat and a dog.

Chapter 7

Sometimes you will read a sentence and feel it needs a pause. Just remember your comma rules. Don't place a comma where it doesn't belong.

Take a look at these sample questions.

1. Ivan wants to win the student government <u>election, but, he is afraid</u> he won't get enough votes.

   A. NO CHANGE
   B. election but, he is afraid
   C. election; but he is afraid
   D. election, but he is afraid

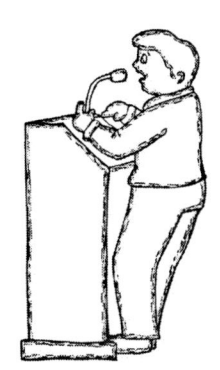

The best answer is D. There needs to be a comma before the coordinating conjunction *but* to connect the two independent clauses. There does not need to be a comma after *but*. Also, if *but* is going to be used, then a semicolon is not the correct punctuation.

2. <u>Reyna, my pretty and popular neighbor, invited</u> me to her party this weekend.

   F. NO CHANGE
   G. Reyna, my pretty, and popular neighbor invited
   H. Reyna, my pretty and popular, neighbor invited
   J. Reyna my pretty, and popular neighbor, invited

The best answer is F. The sentence is correct; the phrase "my pretty and popular neighbor" is the nonrestrictive element that needs to be set off with commas. No additional commas are needed.

3. We were exhausted after a day of trekking <u>up the steep, mountain</u>.

   A. NO CHANGE
   B. up the steep mountain
   C. up, the steep mountain
   D. up, the steep, mountain

The correct answer is B. There is no need for a comma at all in this sentence.

123

Punctuation

APOSTROPHES

Apostrophes are used in many ways, mainly to show possession.

To make singular nouns possessive, add an apostrophe (') and an -*s*.

> **Example:** Sarah's idea was the best among the group.

If a singular noun ends with an *s*, add an apostrophe and an -*s*.

> **Example:** The scheming butler always tried to steal the heiress's fortune.

To make a plural noun ending in *s* possessive, add only the apostrophe.

> **Example:** "You have reached the Beckleys' residence," said the monotone answering machine.

Some words have **irregular plural nouns**. If a plural noun does not end in *s*, the word is made possessive by adding an apostrophe and an -*s*.

> **Example:** A women's gym opened up across the street last month.

To show personal possession by two or more owners, make each noun possessive. To show joint possession of the same object, make only the last noun possessive.

> **Examples:** Rihanna's and Taylor Swift's singing styles are very different.
>
> Dawn and Kent's dad will be coming home from Iraq tomorrow.

COLONS

Use a **colon** to introduce a list, series, quotation, or formal statement. Notice that an independent clause that follows a colon is capitalized.

> **Examples:** We still need the following equipment for the trip: hiking books, backpacks, and a tent.
>
> At some time in your life, you will ask the question: Why do I exist?

Remember, only use a colon after a complete thought when introducing a list.

> **Incorrect Example:** Campers must bring: a flashlight, sleeping bag, and bug spray on the trip next week.

One way to fix this error is to rearrange the sentence to make it a complete thought.

> **Correct Example:** Campers must bring the following items on the trip next week: a flashlight, sleeping bag, and bug spray.

You can also use a colon before a second independent clause that restates or explains the first clause.

> **Example:** The singer had a great voice: every note that she sang was in tune with the music.

124

Use a colon after the greeting in a formal business letter.

>**Examples:** Dear Sir or Madam**:**
>
>To Whom It May Concern**:**

Use a colon to separate chapters and verses in the Bible and other holy scriptures and to separate hours and minutes.

>**Examples:** The answer can be found in Acts 2**:**38.
>
>This movie starts at 2**:**45 p.m.

SEMICOLONS

Semicolons separate independent clauses that are *not* joined by a conjunction. Usually, semicolons are used in place of periods when the two independent clauses are closely related.

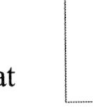

>**Example:** The realtor sold two houses**;** she was very happy that day.

Semicolons separate independent clauses that are joined by sentence interrupters (*for instance, nevertheless, moreover, instead, besides,* and so on.).

>**Example:** The people were panicking in the streets**;** nevertheless, the ambulance was able to move through the crowds.

Semicolons are sometimes used to split independent clauses when there are several commas inside the clauses.

>**Example:** Mr. Trump, a writer, announced his new horror, mystery, and science fiction series**;** yet the books, oddly enough, had not been written.

Semicolons are used if a colon precedes items in a series or if items in a list already use internal commas.

>**Example:** These athletes were all participating in the national competition: Judy Dawes, a world class diver**;** Joe Chung, a champion weight lifter**;** and Sherry Whittaker, an Olympic gymnast.

To review where and how commas, as well as apostrophes, semicolons, and colons, are used as internal punctuation, consult your English textbook or a grammar guide recommended by your teacher.

Punctuation

Practice 2: Internal Punctuation

Directions: Some portions in the following passage have been underlined and numbered. The matching questions in the right-hand column offer alternatives for the underlined portion. You can choose one of these, or select NO CHANGE if the original version in the passage is best. If a number appears in a box within the text, the corresponding question will ask about a section of the text that is not underlined (such as a whole paragraph). To choose the best answer for any question, you should read more than just the underlined portion.

Jack-o'-Lantern Mushroom

The jack-o'-lantern mushroom is a <u>fungus that grows in wooded parts of North America.</u>
                    1
<u>This mushroom which grows in cluster</u>
                    2
<u>formations mainly on decaying trees gets its name from its distinctive appearance.</u> Much like the jack-o'-lanterns people use to decorate in the fall, the jack-o'-lantern mushroom is bright orange or yellow.

1. **A.** NO CHANGE
   B. Fungus, that grows in wooded parts of North America
   C. fungus that grows, in wooded parts of North America
   D. fungus that grows in wooded, parts of North America

2. **F.** NO CHANGE
   G. This mushroom which grows, in cluster formations mainly on decaying trees, gets its name from its distinctive appearance.
   H. This mushroom, which grows in cluster formations mainly on decaying trees, gets its name from its distinctive appearance.
   J. This mushroom which grows in cluster formations, mainly on decaying trees gets its name, from its distinctive appearance.

Besides its bright color the jack-o'-lantern mushroom shares another trait with the popular decoration, it glows. Jack-o'-lantern mushrooms can bioluminesce, which is the ability of living organisms to emit light. Jack-o'-lantern mushrooms are an interesting natural marvel, they are also poisonous and can make people very ill.

3.
- A. NO CHANGE
- B. Besides its bright, color the jack-o'-lantern
- C. Besides its bright, color, the jack-o'-lantern
- D. Besides its bright color, the jack-o'-lantern

4.
- F. NO CHANGE
- G. decoration: It glows
- H. decoration: it glows
- J. decoration; It glows

5.
- A. NO CHANGE
- B. interesting, natural marvel; they are also poisonous
- C. interesting natural marvel; they are also poisonous
- D. interesting natural marvel: they are also poisonous

CHAPTER 7 SUMMARY

End punctuation includes the **period, question mark,** and **exclamation point**.

Internal punctuation includes **commas, apostrophes, semicolons,** and **colons**.

Review the rules of how to use each of these punctuation marks. Focus on the meaning of the passage and the relationship of words, phrases, and clauses to one another.

CHAPTER 7 REVIEW

Directions: Some portions in the following passage have been underlined and numbered. The matching questions in the right-hand column offer alternatives for the underlined portion. You can choose one of these, or select NO CHANGE if the original version in the passage is best. If a number appears in a box within the text, the corresponding question will ask about a section of the text that is not underlined (such as a whole paragraph). To choose the best answer for any question, you should read more than just the underlined portion.

Let's Go Bowling!

The distinctive aromas of paste wax and crinkle-cut french fries mix with the clatter of falling bowling pins. You step up to the <u>lanes</u> edge to take your turn. You pick up your bowling ball, feeling the weight in your hands as you approach the foul line. <u>Sizing up the shot, you draw your arm</u> back, and then you swing and release <u>the hard heavy rubber ball</u>. You can feel the gentle rumble under your feet as the ball rolls over the golden wood lane toward the waiting pins. <u>Then it hits them, and all ten pins, go down.</u>

1. **A.** NO CHANGE
   B. lane's
   C. lanes'
   D. lanes's

2. **F.** NO CHANGE
   G. Sizing up the shot you draw your arm
   H. Sizing up the shot; you draw your arm
   J. Sizing up, the shot, you draw your arm

3. **A.** NO CHANGE
   B. the hard heavy, rubber ball
   C. the hard, heavy rubber, ball
   D. the hard, heavy rubber ball

4. **F.** NO CHANGE
   G. Then, it hits them and all ten pins go down.
   H. Then it hits them, and all ten pins go down.
   J. Then it hits them and, all ten pins, go down.

129

Punctuation

<u>Strike</u> The crowd goes wild!
    5

    This is a regular activity for many lovers of bowling today. But times are changing. You needn't run to your local bowling alley and rent special shoes just to bowl a few frames anymore. Thanks to modern gaming <u>technology, you can flip on your television, and pop a game of video bowling</u> into your
                  6
game system. Will you head to the local bowling alley for a pick-up game of tenpins, or will you pick up your joystick and sit down in front of the <u>TV</u> Before you decide, think
                7
about the differences between bowling and video bowling. <u>Each requires different equipment builds different skills and has different dangers.</u> At least when you play
                8
video bowling, you won't drop a ten-pound ball on your poor toes!

5. **A.** NO CHANGE
   B. Strike.
   C. Strike?
   D. Strike!

6. **F.** NO CHANGE
   G. technology, you can flip on your television and pop a game of video bowling
   H. technology, you can flip on your television and, pop a game of video bowling
   J. technology you can flip on your television and pop a game of video bowling

7. **A.** NO CHANGE
   B. TV.
   C. TV?
   D. TV!

8. **F.** NO CHANGE
   G. Each requires: different equipment, builds different skills, and has different dangers.
   H. Each requires, different equipment, builds different skills and has different dangers.
   J. Each requires different equipment, builds different skills, and has different dangers.

Practice Test 1

30 Minutes – 50 Questions

Directions: Read the following passages. In each passage, certain words and phrases are underlined and numbered. In the right-hand column, you will find alternative choices for the underlined part. Choose the answer that best expresses the idea, makes the statement appropriate for standard written English, or is worded most consistently with the style and tone of the passage as a whole. If you think the original version is best, choose NO CHANGE. In some cases, there will be in the right-hand column a question about the underlined part. Choose the best answer to the question.

There might also be questions about a section of the passage or about the passage as a whole. These questions do not refer to an underlined portion of the passage; they are identified by a number or numbers in a box.

For each question, choose the best answer, and circle the corresponding letter of your answer. Remember that for many of the questions, you must read several sentences beyond the question to determine the answer. Be sure that you have read far enough ahead each time you choose an answer.

Practice Test 1

Putting Your Best Foot Forward

[1]

When people travel to another country, we expect to see differences in foods clothing and living conditions. Indeed, some people don't know how to act. Problems have arisen when people of other lands have misunderstood our words or gestures. We all need to realize that some actions are taken differently in various parts of the world.

[2]

Some things that Americans find innocent are considered rude. In another country or culture. For example, many Americans stand with their hands in their pockets while conversing with friends. Maybe we're lucky enough to find some cash in our pockets. In countries, including Belgium, Indonesia, France, Finland, Japan,

1. **A.** NO CHANGE
   B. they
   C. us
   D. you

2. **F.** NO CHANGE
   G. in, foods, clothing, and, living conditions
   H. in: foods, clothing, and living conditions
   J. in foods, clothing, and living conditions

3. **A.** NO CHANGE
   B. arised
   C. arose
   D. arise

4. **F.** NO CHANGE
   G. are considered rude; in another country or culture.
   H. are considered rude, in another country or culture.
   J. are considered rude in another country or culture.

5. **A.** NO CHANGE
   B. countries; including
   C. countries including
   D. countries: including

132

Practice Test 1

and Sweden, talking with your hands in your pockets is considered <u>discourteous and rude, making people think you are rude</u>. You don't want people to think you don't respect them.

[7]

[3]

In the United States, <u>whistling is not a big deal</u>. In Europe, whistling is used when a person is jeering or heckling a speaker. Also, in India it is considered rude to whistle in public.

[4]

In the States, you may give people directions by pointing your index finger toward the way they should go. To avoid rudeness in Japan and China, you <u>should have pointed</u> with your entire hand—but in Malaysia, you should point with your thumb.

6. F. NO CHANGE
   G. discourteously rude
   H. rude and impolite
   J. discourteous

7. Which sentence in Paragraph 2 should be deleted because it is irrelevant?
   A. Some things that Americans find innocent are considered rude.
   B. For example, many Americans stand with their hands in their pockets while conversing with friends.
   C. Maybe we're lucky enough to find some cash in our pockets.
   D. You don't want people to think you don't respect them.

8. F. NO CHANGE
   G. whistling is a fairly innocent activity
   H. everyone whistles a tune here or there
   J. you can whistle anywhere you want

9. A. NO CHANGE
   B. pointed
   C. should point
   D. are pointing

[5]

Speaking of thumbs, in Germany, the fist with the thumb pointed up is the signal for the number one. In Japan, the same hand signal means the number five. In America and England, that gesture means "okay" or "good job." [10]

[6]

If you're planning a trip to another country, be sure to do a little research.

Eventually, you can avoid unintentional
    11   12

being rude while you are there.
                                13

10. In Paragraph 5, the author wants to add this sentence:

   You can see now how people can be confused by simple hand gestures.

   This sentence would most logically fit into the paragraph as:

   F. as the first sentence.
   G. as the second sentence.
   H. as the third sentence.
   J. as the last sentence.

11. A. NO CHANGE
    B. Meanwhile
    C. Then
    D. This time

12. F. NO CHANGE
    G. unintentionally
    H. unintended
    J. unintendedly

13. A. NO CHANGE
    B. their
    C. they're
    D. theyre

Practice Test 1

The Beginning of Hollywood

[1]

In the beginning, movies had no sound and <u>uncomplicatedly simple</u> plots. Often a silent film lasted only fifteen minutes. The first popular western movie, *The Great Train Robbery*, had three small scenes: a train robbery, a pursuit on horseback, and a surprise ending where the bandit points his gun at the movie audience and fires. [15]

[2]

During the early 1900s, Hollywood and New Jersey were competitors for the movie industry. New Jersey was desirable because so many actors and actresses worked in the theaters of Broadway in nearby New York. However, all filming had to take place outside where the light was strong enough. <u>Regardless</u>, Hollywood, nestled in the hills of sunny Southern California, <u>were</u> more advantageous for year-round filming.

14. F. NO CHANGE
    G. uncomplicated simple
    H. simply uncomplicated
    J. uncomplicated

15. What sentence best introduces the first paragraph?
    A. I'll bet you like movies as much as I do—I watch them every week.
    B. From as early as the 1920s, millions of Americans were regular moviegoers.
    C. Westerns are a movie genre that used to be popular, but not so much now.
    D. Evidently, shoot-'em-up cowboy movies existed back in the early twentieth century.

16. F. NO CHANGE
    G. As a result
    H. Similarly
    J. Then

17. A. NO CHANGE
    B. are
    C. was
    D. is

[3]

By the 1920s, Hollywood had become a booming industry. Making $10,000 per week instead of a few dollars per day, Hollywood paid actors such as Charlie Chaplin better than Broadway did. Directors began producing longer movies with more complicated plots. In time, Hollywood stood for films and the rich, snobby people who starred in them.

18. F. NO CHANGE
    G. Actors such as Charlie Chaplin were making $10,000 per week in Hollywood instead of a few dollars per day on Broadway.
    H. Hollywood paid actors such as Charlie Chaplin better than Broadway did, making $10,000 per week instead of a few dollars per day.
    J. Hollywood, making $10,000 per week instead of a few dollars per day, paid actors such as Charlie Chaplin better than Broadway did.

19. A. NO CHANGE
    B. aloof
    C. sophisticated
    D. nonchalant

[4]

The years between 1920 and 1950 are often referred for as the Golden Age of Hollywood when the film industry was at its peak.

20. F. NO CHANGE
    G. to
    H. by
    J. on

21. A. NO CHANGE
    B. Golden Age of Hollywood when the film industry,
    C. Golden Age, of Hollywood, when the film industry
    D. Golden Age of Hollywood, when the film industry

Practice Test 1

The most popular movies were westerns, romantic comedies, and cartoons. The big studios like MGM, and Paramount, built their empires during this era, or classics like *Casablanca, Citizen Kane, It's a Wonderful Life, The Wizard of Oz*, and many others were created during this time.

22. F. NO CHANGE
    G. big studios, like MGM, and Paramount, built
    H. big studios like MGM and Paramount built
    J. big studios, like MGM and Paramount, built

23. A. NO CHANGE
    B. yet
    C. and
    D. for

Questions 24 and 25 ask about the preceding passage as a whole.

24. What is the main topic of the passage?
    F. Film legend Charlie Chaplin was a central figure of this era.
    G. Actors were better off in Hollywood than on Broadway because they could make more money.
    H. The first half of the twentieth century saw the start and growth of the Hollywood film business.
    J. Movies used to be really simple, but now they have complicated plots and better special effects.

25. Suppose that the writer wanted to add the following sentence to the essay:

    By 1911, fifteen film companies had made California their home.

    This sentence would most logically fit into:
    A. the end of Paragraph 1.
    B. the beginning of Paragraph 2.
    C. the end of Paragraph 2.
    D. the end of Paragraph 3.

Practice Test 1

How to Save a Life

[1]

In many movies and TV shows, you see the hero giving an unconscious victim mouth-to-mouth resuscitation and chest compressions. This emergency procedure, called cardiopulmonary resuscitation (CPR), keeps oxygen-rich blood pumping through the body until medical professionals take over the <u>victims</u> care. CPR can save lives; <u>thus</u>, less than a third of people who have a heart attack receive the <u>immediate CPR that they need right away</u>.

[2]

<u>Why are people so hesitant when it comes to giving CPR?</u>

26. F. NO CHANGE
    G. victims'
    H. victim's
    J. victimes'

27. A. NO CHANGE
    B. however
    C. in addition
    D. incidentally

28. F. NO CHANGE
    G. immediate CPR, right away, that they need
    H. immediate CPR that they need pronto
    J. immediate CPR that they need

29. The author is considering deleting this sentence from the essay. Knowing the focus of the passage, should the author remove this sentence?

    A. Yes, because the question is insensitive to rescue care providers.
    B. Yes, because no one can answer this question with any certainty.
    C. No, because it introduces the topic of the second paragraph.
    D. No, because removing the sentence would make the paragraph look too short.

138

Many of us should of taken first aid courses
                30
in school or become certified in CPR to work as lifeguards or babysitters. However, some people worry that in an emergency, they might forget the steps. When put to the test, he stood back and thought, "I wish I could
           31
help, but I'm afraid I'd do it wrong." Other people are afraid of being sued if the victim kicks the bucket. [33]
        32

30. F. NO CHANGE
    G. should have taken
    H. should have took
    J. should of took

31. A. NO CHANGE
    B. she stood back and thought
    C. we stand back and think
    D. they stand back and think

32. F. NO CHANGE
    G. croaks
    H. doesn't survive
    J. bites the dust

33. What sentence could you add to the end of Paragraph 2 to illustrate the fact that people are afraid to provide CPR?

    A. Still others just don't want to put their mouths over a stranger's and risk getting a disease.
    B. It's a shame that people just don't want to help because they're too busy.
    C. CPR may be important, but it's not as important as avoiding bad foods that give you heart problems.
    D. Would you give a stranger CPR if there were no one else nearby to help?

Practice Test 1

[3]

As a result, the American Heart Association has started endorsing a hands-only form of CPR that is just as effective as the traditional kind. This simplified version of CPR is supposed to make it easy for anyone to jump in, and begin, chest compressions right away. You don't need to do rescue breaths at all—the victim already has enough oxygen in his system, and pausing chest compressions to breathe into their mouth actually stalls the blood circulation. Quick, firm chest compressions—to the beat of the Bee Gees' song "Stayin' Alive"—are sufficient to keep his organs supplied with oxygen until help arrives.

34. F. NO CHANGE
G. to jump in, and begin chest compressions
H. to jump in and begin chest compressions
J. to jump in and begin, chest compressions

35. A. NO CHANGE
B. his
C. your
D. its

[4]

[1] For infants, children, and drowning victims, the traditional combination of rescue breaths and chest compressions is the best way to provide care. [2] However, this new technique works only when the victim is an adult suffering a heart attack, who loses his pulse. [3] With the right knowledge, you could potentially save a life. [4] The new hands-only CPR is effective because it's easy to remember the steps: call 911, and then start pumping that chest! 37

36. F. NO CHANGE
G. However, this new technique works only when the victim is an adult suffering, who loses his pulse, a heart attack.
H. However, this new technique works only when the victim is an adult who loses his pulse during a heart attack.
J. However, this new technique works only when the victim is an adult suffering a heart attack that loses his pulse.

37. In Paragraph 4, which of the following sequences of sentences makes the most logical sense?
A. NO CHANGE
B. 1, 3, 2, 4
C. 4, 2, 1, 3
D. 3, 1, 4, 2

Practice Test 1

The Man Behind Valentine's Day

[1]

Valentine's Day approaches, and here comes the pink hearts with frilly lace edges, bow-and-arrow-toting cupids, and flowers. In schools, young children decorate slotted boxes and deliver valentine cards to all their classmates. By the time you reach high school, you and your friends may have dates on Valentine's Day. The holiday has become one day of the year on which it's acceptable to be romantic and mushy and affectionate with that special someone. Valentine's Day is such a big holiday, in fact, that it comes in second after Christmas as the day the most cards are sent. But Valentine's Day was originally a holy day, a day set aside by the Catholic Church to celebrate the real-life man behind all these traditions and rituals, Saint Valentine.

38. F. NO CHANGE
    G. coming
    H. came
    J. come

39. A. NO CHANGE
    B. that we celebrate it every year with pink-frosted cupcakes
    C. and it takes place in February, a cold month
    D. that many people are frustrated when they can't get a table at a restaurant

[2]

Saint Valentine is believed to have lived in third-century Rome, where Christians were regularly persecuted for their beliefs. After Emperor Claudius II banned marriage in an effort to keep his young men focused and ready for war, <u>mens and womans</u> hearts were broken. According to legends, Valentine was jailed and martyred for secretly marrying young lovers who couldn't bear to be kept apart. One story even sets Valentine as <u>the first person to send a valentine message to someone, while imprisoned and awaiting execution, he sent a letter</u> to a young girl <u>whom</u> visited him, signing it "From your Valentine" at the end. It's no wonder that such a romantic figure, tragically martyred for upholding the virtues of love and devotion, would become a popular saint in England and France during the Middle Ages.

40. F. NO CHANGE
  G. man's and woman's
  H. men's and women's
  J. mens' and womens'

41. A. NO CHANGE
  B. the first person to send a valentine message to someone; while imprisoned and awaiting execution, he sent a letter
  C. the first person to send a valentine message to someone while imprisoned and awaiting execution, he sent a letter
  D. the first person to send a valentine message to someone … while imprisoned and awaiting execution, he sent a letter

42. F. NO CHANGE
  G. whose
  H. which
  J. who

[3]

Nevertheless, the actual holiday (the saint's religious feast day) was set in mid-February to commemorate the honored date of Valentine's death, which occurred around AD 270. However, some scholars believe, that the Church also wished to christianize an ancient Roman festival, known as Lupercalia which took place on February 15.

43. A. NO CHANGE
    B. Anyway
    C. Instead
    D. Thus

44. F. NO CHANGE
    G. commemorate the date
    H. commemorate and honor the date
    J. respectfully commemorate the date

45. A. NO CHANGE
    B. However some scholars believe that the Church also wished to christianize an ancient Roman festival, known as Lupercalia which took place on February 15.
    C. However, some scholars believe, that the Church also wished to christianize an ancient Roman festival, known as Lupercalia, which took place on February 15.
    D. However, some scholars believe that the Church also wished to christianize an ancient Roman festival, known as Lupercalia, which took place on February 15.

This pagan holiday celebrated the coming of spring with a ritualized "spring cleaning" of the home and honored Faunus later associated with Pan the Roman god of fertility and agriculture. 47

46. F. NO CHANGE
G. Faunus, later associated with Pan the Roman god
H. Faunus, later associated with Pan, the Roman god
J. Faunus later associated with Pan the Roman, god

47. What sentence would best conclude Paragraph 3?
A. NO CHANGE
B. Christians eliminated some of the pagan practices, such as the pairing of young men and women through a lottery system.
C. Pan was actually a god from Greek mythology known for having the legs and horns of a goat and whose angry shouts startled people, bringing us the word *panic*.
D. Spring is the best time of the year to clean the house, because it's finally warm enough to open the windows and air out the home.

[4]

[1] By the mid-1840s, these cards were being mass-produced, today about one billion valentines are exchanged each year.

[2] Valentine's Day takes on a life of its own over the centuries. [3] The next time you eat a handful of tiny heart candies inscribed with phrases like "Be Mine" and "Sweet Pea," maybe you'll remember the third-century saint who died for love. [4] By the early 1700s, Americans as well as Europeans were celebrating the special day by exchanging handmade cards. 50

48. F. NO CHANGE
G. these cards were being mass-produced; and today about one billion valentines are exchanged
H. these cards were being mass-produced. But today about one billion valentines are exchanged
J. these cards were being mass-produced, and today about one billion valentines are exchanged

49. A. NO CHANGE
B. will take
C. will have taken
D. has taken

50. Which of the following sequences of sentences will make Paragraph 4 flow most logically?
F. NO CHANGE
G. 2, 4, 1, 3
H. 4, 2, 3, 1
J. 1, 4, 2, 3

Practice Test 2

PLAN ENGLISH
Test Preparation Guide

30 Minutes – 50 Questions

Directions: Read the following passages. In each passage, certain words and phrases are underlined and numbered. In the right-hand column, you will find alternative choices for the underlined part. Choose the answer that best expresses the idea, makes the statement appropriate for standard written English, or is worded most consistently with the style and tone of the passage as a whole. If you think the original version is best, choose NO CHANGE. In some cases, there will be in the right-hand column a question about the underlined part. Choose the best answer to the question.

There might also be questions about a section of the passage or about the passage as a whole. These questions do not refer to an underlined portion of the passage; they are identified by a number or numbers in a box.

For each question, choose the best answer, and circle the corresponding letter of your answer. Remember that for many of the questions, you must read several sentences beyond the question to determine the answer. Be sure that you have read far enough ahead each time you choose an answer.

Practice Test 2

You've Been Flamingoed!

[1]

What's pink and hangs out in your grandma's yard or maybe even <u>you're</u> own
                                                                    1
yard? Yes, it's the <u>all-American, favorite—</u>
                                   2
flamingos! Well, at least the plastic ones.

[2]

The <u>bright</u> colored lawn ornaments were
        3
first made in 1957; <u>they immediately became</u>
                                   4
<u>a symbol of the entire decade</u>. They are sold in sets of two, and since their creation, more than twenty million sets have been sold by the original manufacturer of lawn flamingos.

1. **A.** NO CHANGE
   B. your
   C. youre
   D. your'e

2. **F.** NO CHANGE
   G. all-American: favorite
   H. all-American; favorite
   J. all-American favorite

3. **A.** NO CHANGE
   B. brighter
   C. brightly
   D. brightest

4. The author is considering deleting this clause from the essay. Based on the focus and purpose of the essay, should the author make this revision?
   F. Yes, because it's an implausible statement that can't be proved.
   G. No, because it's relevant to the history and popularity of the pink flamingo.
   H. No, because people generally like objects from the 1950s.
   J. Yes, because poodle skirts and drive-in burger joints are better symbols of the decade.

Practice Test 2

[3]

Something about the birds puts a smile on people's faces. In the 1990s, putting a whole flock of pink plastic birds in someone's yard became one of the <u>hilariousest</u> practical jokes around. People could pay to have a <u>friend's yard "flamingoed." Whereas the intended victims</u> were not helpless. They could buy "flamingo insurance," and even if a friend had paid to have the victim's yard flamingoed, the insurance policy would prevent the surprise flamingo show from taking place! [7]

5. **A.** NO CHANGE
   B. hilariouser
   C. most hilarious
   D. more hilariouser

6. **F.** NO CHANGE
   G. friend's yard "flamingoed" and the intended victims
   H. friend's yard "flamingoed," so the intended victims
   J. friend's yard "flamingoed," but the intended victims

7. In Paragraph 3, the author wants to add this sentence:

   In fact, one club used that amusing caper as a fundraising project.

   This sentence would most logically fit as:

   A. the first sentence.
   B. the second sentence.
   C. the third sentence.
   D. the fourth sentence.

[4]

Aside from lawns, drawings of flamingos show up in all sorts of places. You could see images of flamingos with their distinctive long necks and legs hanging in tropical-themed restaurants and printed on Hawaiian-style shirts. Pictures of flamingos adorn everything from glassware to totebags. Souvenirs with flamingos on it are popular collector's items.

[5]

Although one species of flamingo is extinct in the wild in North America, no longer alive, many types of live flamingos can be seen in bird sanctuaries zoos and the gardens of fancy resort, hotels. The plastic ones are everywhere!

8. F. NO CHANGE
   G. can
   H. could have
   J. canned

9. A. NO CHANGE
   B. images of flamingos, hanging in tropical-themed restaurants, with their distinctive long necks and legs
   C. images of flamingos, with their distinctive long necks and legs, hanging in tropical-themed restaurants
   D. images, with their distinctive long necks and legs hanging, of flamingos in tropical-themed restaurants

10. F. NO CHANGE
    G. them
    H. him
    J. us

11. A. NO CHANGE
    B. is extinct in the wild in North America and no longer alive
    C. is extinct in the wild, no longer alive in North America
    D. is extinct in the wild in North America

12. F. NO CHANGE
    G. in: bird, sanctuaries, zoos and the gardens of fancy resort hotels
    H. in, bird sanctuaries, zoos, and the gardens of fancy, resort, hotels
    J. in bird sanctuaries, zoos, and the gardens of fancy resort hotels

Practice Test 2

East Meets West

[1]

One of the most popular adaptations <u>are</u>
                                      13
the style of dress. Many Japanese today wear "Western" style clothing such as business suits, activewear, jeans, and T-shirts. <u>Traditional clothing which goes back</u>
                                14
<u>hundreds of years</u> is often reserved for special occasions. ☐15

13. **A.** NO CHANGE
    B. is
    C. were
    D. was

14. **F.** NO CHANGE
    G. Traditional clothing which goes back, hundreds of years,
    H. Traditional clothing, which goes back hundreds of years,
    J. Traditional, clothing which goes back hundreds, of years

15. What sentence best introduces Paragraph 1?

    A. Japan, an East Asian island, is located in the Pacific Ocean next to China, Russia, North Korea, and South Korea.
    B. Japan is an archipelago, or collection of islands, that consists of 6,852 islands.
    C. It is amazing how the Japanese have retained their cultural heritage while simultaneously integrating many aspects of Western culture.
    D. Japan is going through some changes while also staying the same.

151

Practice Test 2

[2]

Many Japanese also have adopted Western furnishings into their homes. Western influences, which throughout Japanese popular culture, include fast-food restaurants, music, and the movies.
<u>_____</u>
16

[3]

The Japanese also have more time to devote to relaxed leisure. According by studies, spending time with family, friends,
17   18
home improvement, shopping, and gardening form the mainstream of leisure, together with sports and travel. The number of Japanese making overseas trips has increased a whole
19
bunch in recent years. Meanwhile, domestic
                         20
travel, picnics, hiking, and cultural events rank high among favorite activities.

[4]

Japan is a land with a vibrant and fascinating history, varied culture, traditions, and customs who are hundreds of years old,
21

16. F. NO CHANGE
    G. which heavily throughout Japanese popular culture
    H. which in Japanese popular culture
    J. which can be seen throughout Japanese popular culture

17. A. NO CHANGE
    B. relax
    C. leisure
    D. relaxing leisure

18. F. NO CHANGE
    G. to
    H. under
    J. in

19. A. NO CHANGE
    B. notably
    C. lots
    D. bigly

20. F. NO CHANGE
    G. At once
    H. Eventually
    J. First

21. A. NO CHANGE
    B. that
    C. whom
    D. whose

152

Practice Test 2

<u>for</u> segments of its society and economy are
22
as new as the microchips in a personal

computer.

22. **F.** NO CHANGE
    G. or
    H. yet
    J. and

Questions 23 and 24 ask about the preceding passage as a whole.

23. Which sentence best states the main idea of the passage?

    A. In Japan, you will find evidence of traditional customs and culture as well as examples of Western-style adaptations.

    B. In Japan, jeans, fast food, picnics, and personal computers are very popular.

    C. In Japan, people always enjoy traveling overseas and shopping.

    D. Japanese and American cultures are so similar that you really cannot tell the difference between them.

24. Suppose that the writer wanted to add the following sentence to the essay:

    It is not unusual to have a completely westernized home with only one room decorated in the traditional Japanese style.

    This sentence would most logically fit into:

    F. the beginning of Paragraph 1.
    G. the end of Paragraph 2.
    H. the end of Paragraph 3.
    J. the beginning of Paragraph 4.

153

The 400 Blows and the French New Wave

[1]

Directors of the French New Wave, a film movement that blossomed between 1959 and 1963, blended realism with artistry in their films. Borrowing techniques from Italian films made after World War II; New Wave directors like Francois Truffaut and Jean-Luc Godard often shot on location and used nonprofessional actors. According to the *auteur* theory, it was the director not the screenwriter who was the author, of the film, using the camera much like the way a writer uses a pen to tell a story. The 1959 film *The 400 Blows*, directed by Truffaut, is a famous example of the French New Wave.

25. A. NO CHANGE
    B. after World War II, New Wave directors
    C. after World War II: New Wave directors
    D. after World War II. New Wave directors

26. F. NO CHANGE
    G. it was the director, not the screenwriter who was the author of the film, using the camera much like the way a writer uses a pen, to tell a story
    H. it was the director, not the screenwriter, who was the author of the film, using the camera much like the way a writer uses a pen to tell a story
    J. it was the director not the screenwriter who was the author of the film using the camera much like the way a writer uses a pen to tell a story

[2]

[1] Truffaut based the character on himself, drawing on experiences and challenges he faced in his youth. [2] Ignored by his parents and frequently in trouble at school, Antoine begins a life of petty crime. [3] The protagonist of *The 400 Blows* is a twelve-year-old boy named Antoine, who lives with his mother and stepfather in a small Parisian apartment. [4] <u>The boy is eventually arrested after he's caught from his dad's office stealing a typewriter.</u> 28

[3]

The <u>famous concluding scene of the movie comes at the end</u>, when Antoine makes a desperate bid for freedom. Fleeing the reform school to which <u>they were sent, they ran</u> indefatigably down a long road all the way to the edge of a desolate beach.

27. **A.** NO CHANGE
    B. The boy is eventually arrested from his dad's office after he's caught stealing a typewriter.
    C. From his dad's office, the boy is eventually arrested after he's caught stealing a typewriter.
    D. The boy is eventually arrested after he's caught stealing a typewriter from his dad's office.

28. In Paragraph 2, which of the following sequences of sentences is the most logical?
    F. NO CHANGE
    G. 3, 1, 2, 4
    H. 4, 1, 2, 3
    J. 1, 3, 4, 2

29. **A.** NO CHANGE
    B. famous concluding scene of the movie comes at the close
    C. most famous scene of the movie comes at the end
    D. famous final scene of the movie comes at the end

30. **F.** NO CHANGE
    G. he was sent, they ran
    H. she was sent, she was running
    J. he has been sent, he runs

It's not clear what beach it is, but it doesn't look like a well-known tourist location. A traditional chase scene as filmed in Hollywood <u>would of cut</u> rapidly between the escapee and his pursuer, but Truffaut has framed it as a long, uninterrupted shot of Antoine running. The scene runs over a minute long; <u>besides</u>, it's effective in terms of drama because it shows the boy's struggle in real time. 33

[4]
With Antoine trapped between the land and the sea, *The 400 Blows* has <u>an unintelligible</u> ending; the camera zooms in on the <u>boys</u> confused face, and then the image freezes.

31. A. NO CHANGE
    B. would of cutted
    C. would have cut
    D. would have cutted

32. F. NO CHANGE
    G. indeed
    H. on the other hand
    J. namely

33. Which sentence in Paragraph 3 should be deleted because it disrupts the flow of the paragraph?
    A. The famous concluding scene of the movie comes at the end, when Antoine makes a desperate bid for freedom.
    B. It's not clear what beach it is, but it doesn't look like a well-known tourist location.
    C. A traditional chase scene as filmed in Hollywood would cut rapidly between the escapee and his pursuer, but Truffaut has framed it as a long, uninterrupted shot of Antoine running.
    D. The scene runs over a minute long; besides, it's effective in terms of drama because it shows the boy's struggle in real time.

34. F. NO CHANGE
    G. an ambiguous
    H. a fishy
    J. a dubious

35. A. NO CHANGE
    B. boys'
    C. boy's
    D. boys's

Practice Test 2

A straightforward resolution doesn't

occur.

> Questions 36 and 37 ask about the preceding passage as a whole.

36. The author is considering adding this sentence to Paragraph 4:

    Does Antoine make it to freedom, or is he taken back to the reform school?

    Should the author make this revision?

    F. Yes, because anyone watching the movie will ask the same question.

    G. Yes, because it emphasizes the point that the film's ending is uncertain.

    H. No, because it disturbs the flow of the final paragraph.

    J. No, because it's never acceptable to have a question in an essay.

37. Which sentence would best conclude the essay?

    A. This was the realism New Wave directors strived for: Not every story has a happy ending.

    B. It's a bad idea to end a film this way, because it will only frustrate the audience.

    C. Because the film is partly autobiographical, Antoine must have become a film director like Truffaut.

    D. A Hollywood ending would be more thrilling because Antoine would get revenge on his parents.

Practice Test 2

The Fleeting Charm of Fads

[1]

Every decade brings with it new fads, trends, and the latest must-have toys or gadgets. In the 1980s, it was Cabbage Patch dolls and Rubik's Cubes. The 1990s saw the booming popularity of Tamagotchi pets and *Mortal Kombat* video games. It seems like some sort of hot new trend is popping up every day. Perhaps fads catch on because people naturally want to be a part of what's popular at the moment. 38

38. Which sentence best introduces the essay?
   F. Something about a fad is irresistible, making children and adults alike feel as if they *must* buy, collect, and trade that hot new item.
   H. Fads are trendy items now, but they'll typically end up in a colorful pile at your next yard sale or in your trash.
   H. Lava lamps were a big sensation in the 1960s and 1970s, but now you're most likely to find them in novelty stores and college dorm rooms.
   J. Only weak-willed people get involved in fads, because they follow the herd mentality; unique people like things that aren't popular.

Practice Test 2

[2]

Next, fervor over a new toy isn't always
pretty. In shopping malls, especially during the holidays, parents have gotten into physical brawls over the last Tickle Me Elmo or Buzz Lightyear doll. During the Beanie Baby craze, when McDonald's started offering "Teenie Beanies" in its Happy Meals, adults swarmed to the drive-throughs in droves. Not all was parents desperate to get

a plush stuffed animal for their children, some were eager collectors amassing these toys in hopes that they'd become rare collector's items, that are worth a tidy fortune, sometime in the future.

39. A. NO CHANGE
B. Finally
C. Similarly
D. However

40. F. NO CHANGE
G. its Happy Meals, and adults
H. its Happy Meals; adults
J. its Happy Meals adults

41. A. NO CHANGE
B. swarmed to the drive-throughs like droves of animals
C. swarmed to the drive-throughs drove-like
D. swarmed to the drive-throughs

42. F. NO CHANGE
G. are
H. were
J. is

43. A. NO CHANGE
B. for their children; some were eager collectors
C. for their children, and some were eager collectors
D. for their children; and some were eager collectors

44. F. NO CHANGE
G. rare collector's items, worth a tidy fortune sometime, in the future
H. rare collector's items worth a tidy fortune sometime in the future
J. rare collector's items, that are worth a tidy fortune sometime in the future

159

So many adults are crestfallen when they discover that their mothers threw away their comic-book collections, which often take years to build up. [45]

[3]

[1] Dolls, marbles, toy dishes, and yo-yos have been around since the earliest days of civilization. [2] Well, they may have been only half serious, but there is something appealing about simple, uncomplicated toys. [3] Did your parents ever joke that when they were children, they had to entertain <u>ourselves</u> with nothing but sticks, pebbles, and pieces of string? [4] It's the toys that spark the imagination and engage the mind that have the most long-lasting value, apparently. [47]

45. Which sentence from Paragraph 2 should be deleted because it is irrelevant?

   A. Next, fervor over a new toy isn't always pretty.
   B. In shopping malls, especially during the holidays, parents have gotten into physical brawls over the last Tickle Me Elmo or Buzz Lightyear doll.
   C. During the Beany Baby craze, when McDonald's started offering "Teenie Beanies" in its Happy Meals, adults swarmed to the drive-throughs in droves.
   D. So many adults are crestfallen when they discover that their mothers threw away their comic-book collections, which often take years to build up.

46. F. NO CHANGE
    G. itself
    H. yourself
    J. themselves

47. Which of the following sequences of sentences improves the coherence and logic of Paragraph 3?

    A. NO CHANGE
    B. 3, 2, 1, 4
    C. 4, 2, 3, 1
    D. 3, 4, 1, 2

[4]

While the latest high-tech gadgets practically screamed to be bought, some of the most popular fads have been remarkably unsophisticated. Pokémon trading cards and pogs were merely pieces of cheap, thin cardboard, after all. The Pet Rock was nothing more than a rock stuck in a straw-filled crate. Most recently, kids clamored for cleverly shaped rubber bands to wear on their wrists. To make a long story short, these in-vogue items' attraction to people seems to last only approximately one or two years, give or take. Even if these faddish items never pay for your grandchildrens' college tuition, they're still fun while they last.

48. F. NO CHANGE
    G. were screaming
    H. scream
    J. screams

49. A. NO CHANGE
    B. To make a long story short, the attraction of these items for people seems to last only roughly one or two years.
    C. To be succinct, these in-vogue items' appeal to people appears to last only about one or two years, more or less.
    D. However, the appeal of these trendy items rarely lasts more than a couple of years.

50. F. NO CHANGE
    G. grandchilds'
    H. grandchildren's
    J. grandchildrens

Practice Test 2

A
action verb 94, 112
adjective 105, 112
adjective clause 87
adverb 50, 51, 54, 105, 112
antecedent 100, 102, 112
audience 32, 39
author
   audience 32
   point of view 86
   purpose 25, 32, 39
   style 58, 72
   tone 72
   voice 33

C
cause and effect 48, 50, 54
central idea 26, 39
chronological order 48, 49, 54
clarity (word) 58, 65, 72
classification order 48
clause 77, 79, 87, 90, 102
coherence 47
comma 78
comma splice 79, 90
comparative modifier 105, 112
compare and contrast 48, 50, 54
compound antecedent 102
concluding sentence 44
concrete words 72
conjunction 67, 78
conjunctive adverb 50, 51, 54
connotation 36, 39

D
dangling modifier 83, 90
denotation 36, 39
dependent clause 77, 79, 90
detail 26, 28, 44

E
economy (word) 58, 72

F
faulty coordination 78, 90
focus 39
   of essay 25
   of passage 25
formal voice 33

H
helping verb 94, 112
homonym 109

I
idea
   central idea 26, 39
   main idea 27
   organize 47
idiom 107, 112
indefinite-pronoun antecedent 102
independent clause 77, 79, 90
informal voice 33
introductory sentence 44
irregular modifier 106
irregular verb 96, 112

L
linking verb 94, 112

M
main idea 27
misplaced modifier 83, 84, 90
modifier 83, 84, 90, 105, 106
mood 72

O
order of importance 48
organizational pattern 48, 49, 54

P
paragraph 44, 47, 54
participle 95, 97, 112
past participle 112
point of view 90
preposition 107, 112
prepositional phrase 107
present participle 112
problem and solution 48
pronoun 101, 102
pronoun case 100, 112
pronoun-antecedent agreement 102

R
reflexive pronoun 101, 112
relative clause 102, 112
relative pronoun 87, 102, 112
relevant detail 28

S
sentence
   complex 78, 90
   compound 78, 90
   compound-complex 78, 90
   concluding 44
   construction 86, 90
   fragment 79
   fused 78, 90
   introductory 44
   meaning 78, 83
   run-on 78, 90
   simple 77, 90
sequence of events 49, 54
style (word) 58
subject-verb agreement 97, 112
subordination 79, 90
superlative modifier 105, 106, 112
supporting detail 26, 39

T
time order 49, 54
tone (word) 58
topic development 26, 39
transition 43, 47, 49, 50, 54

V
verb 94, 96, 112
verb phrase 94
verb tense 86, 90, 95, 112
voice 33

W
word choice 57, 60, 72
wordiness 69, 72